Berlitz® speaking your langu

Mandarin Chinese

in 30 days

Course Book

by De-an Wu Swihart

Berlitz® speaking your language

Mandarin Chinese *in 30 days*

Course Book

by De-an Wu Swihart

Berlitz Publishing
New York London Singapore

Contacting the Editors

Every effort has been made to provide accurate information in this publication, but changes are inevitable. The publisher cannot be responsible for any resulting loss, inconvenience or injury. We would appreciate it if readers would call our attention to any errors or outdated information, please contact us at: comments@berlitzpublishing.com

Original edition: 2001 by Langenscheidt KG, Berlin and Munich

Second Edition
Printed in China 2015

Senior Commissioning Editor: Kate Drynan
Design: Beverley Speight
Picture research: Beverley Speight

Cover photos: © All Ming Tang Evans except Ryan Pyle doorknocker; and spinach dish

Interior photos: © All Brice Minnight except David Henley p27, 150, 161, 179, 212, 224; Alex Havret p67, 72, 82, 86, 93, 155, 186; Ming Tang Evans p114; Beverley Speight p132; Britta Jaschinski p138; iStockphoto p102, 107, 127

Distribution

Worldwide
APA Publications GmbH & Co. Verlag KG
(Singapore branch)
7030 Ang Mo Kio Ave 5
08-65 Northstar @ AMK, Singapore 569880
Email: apasin@singnet.com.sg

UK and Ireland
Dorling Kindersley Ltd
(a Penguin Company)
80 Strand, London, WC2R 0RL, UK
Email: sales@uk.dk.com

US
Ingram Publisher Services
One Ingram Blvd, PO Box 3006
La Vergne, TN 37086-1986
Email: ips@ingramcontent.com

Australia
Woodslane
10 Apollo St
Warriewood, NSW 2102
Email: info@woodslane.com.au

Contents

How to Use this Book

Mandarin Chinese in 30 Days is a self-study course which will provide you with a basic knowledge of everyday Mandarin in a very short time. The course is divided into 30 short, manageable daily lessons. This book will familiarize you with the main grammatical structures of Mandarin and provide you with a good command of essential vocabulary. In 30 days you will acquire both an active and a passive understanding of the language, enabling you to function effectively in day-to-day life.

Each chapter is an episode in a journey that takes place over 30 days, from your arrival to your final departure, with the main focus on typical, day-to-day situations. The days follow a similar pattern: first, there is a short intro into what you will learn as well as some country and culture information about China. You will then focus on vocabulary, grammar or exercises to reinforce what you have learned. The Key to Exercises at the back of the book will enable you to check your progress.

Every Day features audio that will help you to progress more quickly in Mandarin. These are marked by a CD symbol. Some Days have several dialogues or audio sections to demonstrate different themes or grammar points. These will follow in the same order that they appear in the book. Finally, at the back of the book, you will find a Vocabulary section with the characters, pinyin and English equivalent. This features all the vocabulary you will have learned throughout the course and can be used for quick reference or alone to build your vocabulary.

day: 1

Welcome to China

Pinyin is a romanized phonetic writing system for Chinese based on the national standard system of pronunciation. It was officially adopted by the Chinese government in 1958 to help speakers of other dialects learn the standard pronunciation. It has also become the main system of romanization outside of China. It is widely used on street signs, store signs, and in book titles, as well as in books, magazines and newspapers for non-native speakers of Chinese. **Pinyin** is also used to input characters in Chinese computer word-processing systems. **Pinyin** can help English speakers accurately pronounce any Chinese character.

A **Pinyin** syllable has three components: an **initial**, a **final**, and a **tone mark** that indicates the pitch contour. There are twenty-one initials, thirty-eight finals, and four tones.

Pinyin uses all of the English letters (except **v**) to form a phonetic alphabet. In this book, we use English as a point of reference for learning **Pinyin**, but keep in mind that this is only an approximation, as **Pinyin** was not designed solely for English speakers.

Initials

Initials are similar to consonants in English, but English consonants can appear anywhere in a word, not just at the beginning. Initials are always placed at the beginning of a syllable. They can be divided into six groups based on their phonetic characteristics.

b, p, m, f (Labials)

Formed using the lips. Pronounced the same as in English.

b- p- m- f-

d, t, n, l (Dentals)

Formed with the tongue touching or near the back of the upper teeth. Pronounced the same as in English.

d- t- n- l-

g, k, h (Velars)

Formed from the throat. The letters g and k are the same as in English, but h is slightly more guttural or aspirated than the English h and more like the German ch in ach.

g- k- h-

The next three groups are usually more difficult to pronounce for English speakers.

j, q, x (Frontals)

Formed with the tip of the tongue directly against the back of the lower teeth. Unlike English, the tip of the tongue does not touch the roof of the mouth. The tongue curves, with its upper front surface touching just behind the ridge behind the upper teeth. The lips must be tight and pulled widely apart, as in a forced smile.

Frontal	Pronunciation	Example
j-	ji, jee, gee	*Jimmy, jeep*
q-	chee	*cheese, chip*
x-	shee	*ship, sheer*

z, c, s (Aveolars)

Formed with the tip of the tongue touching or near the base of the lower teeth and with the upper teeth in contact with the upper front surface of the tongue. Be alert to avoid the tendency of some English speakers to pronounce c incorrectly as k (instead of as ts).

Aveolar	Pronunciation	Example
z-	z, dz, ds	*kids, woods*
c-	ts	*its, cats, rats*
s-	(same as English)	*sense, step*

zh, ch, sh, r (Retroflexes)

Formed with the tip of the tongue rolled upward and touching the roof of the mouth. When you say r in Chinese the lips should be less open than in English. You will feel the air vibrating around your tongue. Your lower jaw is thrust slightly forward.

Retroflex	Pronunciation	Example
zh-	dj	*bridge*
ch-	ch	*chat*
sh-	sh	*shore*
r-	cross between j and r	no English equivalent

Finals

Finals are composed of up to four letters. All 38 finals are made from six single vowels (a, e, i, o, u, ü), which can be combined with three consonant endings (n, ng, r). All the finals are listed in this chart. Many vowel sounds do not have English equivalents; listen carefully to the pronunciation on the CD.

Final	By itself	Pronunciation	Examples
-a	a	ah	*ah, father*
-ai	ai	i	*rise, my, eye*
-an	an	ahn	*analyze*
-ang	ang	ahng	*gong*
-ao	ao	ow	*how*
-e	e	uh	(no English equivalent)
-ei		ay	*eight, pay*
-en	en	un	*run*
-eng		ung	*pungent*
-er		ur	*car, curve* (cross between "ar" and "er")
-o		similar to Chinese uo (begin with lips puckered; end with lips apart)	*wore, woman*
-ong	awng	(like "wrong" but with rounder o sound)	*Hong Kong*
-ou	ou	oh (begin with lips apart; end with lips puckered)	*go, owe*

Spelling Changes

When i, u, ü Are Semi-Vowels

When the finals i, u, ü (and any compound using i, u, ü, such as ia, uang, üan) are not preceded by an initial, they are called semi-vowels, which means they actually function as initials. In these cases, their spelling changes as shown:

change "i" to "y" when "i" is at the initial position

change "u" to "w" when "w" is at the initial position

change "ü" to "yu" when "ü" is at the initial position

change "i" to "yi" when "i" is by itself

change "u" to "wu" when "u" is by itself

Final	Spelling change	English sound
-i	yi	ee
-ia	ya	ee-ah (said as one syllable)
-ian	yan	ee-en (said as one syllable)
-iang	yang	ee-ahng
-iao	yao	ee-ow (said as one syllable)
-ie	ye	ee-eh (said as one syllable), "i" is shorter and softer than "e"
-in	yin	een
-ing	ying	ing
-iong	yong	ee-ong (said as one syllable)
-iu	yu	e-o (said as one syllable)
-u	wu	oo
-ua	wa	wah
-uai	wai	wai
-uan	wan	wahn
-uang	wang	wahng
-ueng	weng	oo-ung
-ui	wei	way
-un	wen	wun
-uo	wo	no English equivalent, similar to Chinese -o; *wore* (begin with lips puckered out; end with lips apart); *woman*
-ü	yu	like French eu or German ü; no English equivalent; used only after n or l
-üan	yuan	y as in Yvonne plus e; no English equivalent
-üe	yue	weh, oo-eh (said like one syllable); y as in *Yvonne* plus *an*; no English equivalent
-ün	yun	y as in *Yvonne* plus *n*; no English equivalent

Spelling Changes of the Final ü

When ü follows j-, q-, or x- in a syllable, it changes to u, as in these examples:

jü → juan	jue	jun
qü → quan	que	qun
xü → xuan	xue	xun

Tones

Each syllable in Chinese has a tone. In spoken Chinese, changing the tone of a syllable changes its meaning. For instance, qu in the 3rd tone means *"a man marries a woman"*, but qu in the 4th tone means *"to go"*.

The diagrams below illustrate each of the four tones:

1st tone
5-5

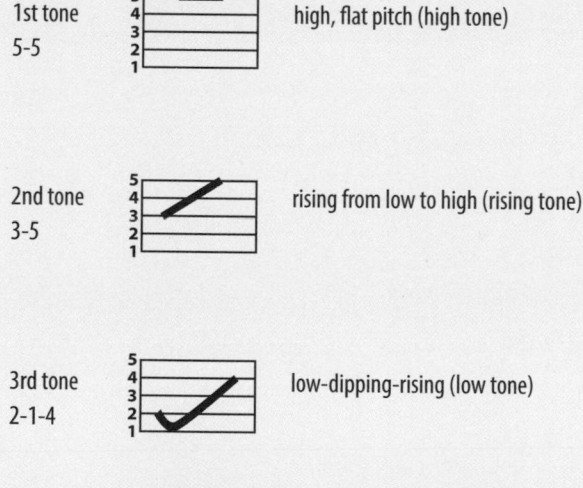

high, flat pitch (high tone)

2nd tone
3-5

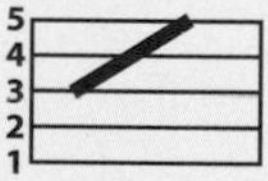

rising from low to high (rising tone)

3rd tone
2-1-4

low-dipping-rising (low tone)

4th tone
5-1

falls from high to low (falling tone)

In the Pinyin system, the tone mark is placed above the vowel. If there are two vowels in a final, the tone mark is placed above the first vowel, except that when the first vowel is **i**, **u**, or **ü**, the tone mark is placed above the second vowel. Examples: **liù**, **duì**, **yuán**. Chinese characters are not written with tone marks.

On the CD you can hear the four different tones of ma.

mā	**má**	**mǎ**	**mà**
妈 *mother*	麻 *hemp*	马 *horse*	骂 *curse*

Neutral Tone

Chinese also has a neutral tone, which has no tone mark and is unstressed. A neutral tone always follows a major-toned syllable and never comes at the beginning of a phrase:

tāde	*his*	(1st tone followed by a neutral tone)
tāmende	*theirs*	(1st tone followed by two neutral tones)

A neutral tone is shorter and lighter than major-toned syllables. However there are two levels of pitch for neutral tones, depending on the tone of the previous syllable:

Low neutral tone

When a neutral tone follows a 1st, 2nd, or 4th tone, it is pronounced in a lower pitch:

gēge	*elder brother*
yéye	*grandfather*

High neutral tone

When a neutral tone follows a 3rd tone, it is pronounced in a higher pitch:

jiějie	*elder sister*
wǎnshang	*evening*

Tone Changes

Yī *(one)*, **qī** *(seven)*, **bā** *(eight)*, **bù** *(no)* can have several different tones. Keep in mind that:

1. **Yī** can have three different tones: 1st (when used alone), 2nd (when before a 4th tone) or 4th (when before a 1st, 2nd or 3rd tone)
2. **Qī** and **bā** each can have two tones: 1st tone or 2nd tone (when followed by a 4th tone).
3. 不 **bù** *(no)* can be 4th tone or 2nd tone (when followed by a 4th tone).

3+3 → 2+3

If a 3rd tone is followed by another 3rd tone, the first 3rd tone is pronounced as a 2nd tone although the printed tone mark does not change:

nǐ hǎo → ní hǎo	*Hello! How do you do!*
hěn měi → hén měi	*very beautiful*

Half-3rd Tone

When a 3rd tone is followed by a 1st, 2nd, or 4th tone, the 3rd tone is pronounced as a half-3rd tone (which only falls but does not rise), although the printed tone mark does not change:

měitiān	*every day*
Měiguó	*America*
mǎipiào	*buy a ticket*

Syllable Division Marks

When a syllable beginning with **a**, **o**, or **e** follows another syllable and could cause confusion about how the syllables should be divided, an apostrophe (') is added in front of the second syllable.

For example: **Xī'ān** (西安 *a city name*)

might be confused with: **xiān** (先 *first*).

Each of the three components of a Chinese syllable — initial, final, and tone — is important. Incorrect pronunciation of any component can result in misunderstanding. Pay careful attention to each syllable's tone and practice the tones now, at the very beginning of your study of Chinese. Doing so will give you a solid foundation for effective communication in Chinese.

day:2

Pronunciation

Day 2 is all about practicing your pronunciation of Chinese and becoming familiar with the different tones and how they affect the meaning of words. Make sure you follow along to the CD for the exercise section to ensure your pronunciation is correct.

中文 ZHŌNGWÉN (THE CHINESE LANGUAGE)...

There are four ways to refer to the Chinese language.
中文 ***Zhōngwén*** *originally referred to the written Chinese language but now generally also includes spoken Chinese. A more precise term for the Chinese language is 汉语* ***Hànyǔ****, which covers both the spoken and the written Chinese. 中国话* ***Zhōngguóhuà*** *is a colloquial term for spoken Chinese.*
普通话 ***Pǔtōnghuà*** *is the official name for Mandarin.*

Grammar

Pronouncing Chinese

For many centuries, in imperial China, **Mandarin** was the official dialect (**Guānhuà** 官话), and was spoken by officials throughout China. However, in 1919 the government designated Mandarin as the "National Language" (**Guóyǔ** 国语), using the Beijing dialect as the standard for pronunciation and the vernacular Northern dialect as the standard for vocabulary and grammar. Since the establishment of the People's Republic of China in 1949, Mandarin has been referred to as "Common Speech" (**Pǔtōnghuà** 普通话); Taiwan has continued to use the name "**Guóyǔ**."

In addition to Mandarin, there are seven other major dialects of Chinese, each of which is native to one or two provinces in southeastern China:

The **Northern** dialect (Běifāng fāngyán 北方方言) (spoken by 73 percent of Chinese people) is spoken in many provinces, including Héběi, Hénán, Shāndōng, Shānxī, Shǎnxī, Yúnnán, Guìzhou, Sìchuān, Ānhuī, Húběi, and northern Jiāngsū.

The **Wú** 吴 dialect (spoken by 8 percent of Chinese people) is spoken in the area around Jiāngsū and Shànghǎi. Wú is the old name of Jiāngsū province.

The **Xiāng** 湘 dialect (spoken by 5 percent of Chinese people) is spoken in and around Húnán province. Xiāng is the old name of Húnán province.

The **Yuè** 粤 dialect, or Cantonese (Guǎngdōnghuà 广东话), (spoken by 5 percent of Chinese people) is spoken in Guǎngdōng, Hong Kong, Macao, Singapore, and by many overseas Chinese around the world.

The **Hakka** dialect (Kèjiāhuà 客家话) (spoken by 4.3 percent of Chinese people) is spoken in Guǎngxī, Fújiàn, Singapore, and Taiwan.

The **Gàn** 赣 dialect (Jiāngxīhuà 江西话) (spoken by 1.7 percent of Chinese people) is spoken in and around Jiāngxī. Gàn is the old name of Jiāngxī province.

The **Mǐn** 闽 dialect is divided into Southern Mǐn and Northern Mǐn dialects. Two percent of Chinese people speak Southern Mǐn; they are in the southern part of Fújiàn province, which is centered around the capital city of Xiàmén, and in Taiwan and Singapore. It is called " Mǐnnánhuà 闽南话" or "Xiàménhuà 厦门话." One percent of Chinese people speak Northern Mǐn; they are in the northern part of Fújiàn, around Fúzhōu.

Exercises

Exercise 1

Pronunciation Practice

Read the following aloud, being careful to pronounce the tones correctly. Refer to the CD to check your pronunciation.

a. The four tones of yi, in order and in reverse order:

yī yí yǐ yì   yì yǐ yí yī

b. The four tones of er:

ér ěr (ēr) èr   ěr èr ér (ēr)

c. sān vs. sǎn:

sān sǎn sǎn sān   sǎn sān sān sǎn

d. sī vs. sì:

sī sì sì sī   sì sī sī sì

e. wǔ vs. wù

wǔ wù wǔ wù   wù wǔ wù wǔ

f. liù vs. liú

liù liú liù liú   liú liù liú liù

g. qī vs. qǐ

qī qǐ qǐ qī   qǐ qī qī qǐ

Exercise 2

Read aloud these common Chinese surnames. Refer to the CD to check your pronunciation. You'll also hear the numbers read in Chinese before each name. You'll learn these in depth later.

1. **Chén**
2. **Dèng**
3. **Féng**

4. Gāo
5. Guō
6. Huáng
7. Jiǎ
8. Jīn
9. Kǒng
10. Lǐ
11. Liáng
12. Lín
13. Liú
14. Mèng
15. Shěn
16. Sūn
17. Tián
18. Wú
19. Xiè
20. Yáng
21. Zhāng
22. Zhào
23. Zhèng
24. Zhōu

Exercise 3

Read the following words aloud, paying special attention to the tones. Refer to the CD to check your pronunciation.

1+1: **fēijī** (airplane) **shāfā** (sofa) **shūbāo** (school bag) **Xiāngshān** (Fragrant Hills) **huāshēng** (peanut)

1+1+1: **Zhījiāgē** (Chicago)

2+2: **Chángchéng** (Great Wall) **shítáng** (cafeteria) **yínháng** (bank)

yóutiáo (fried bread) **Huánghé** (Yellow River)

2+2+2: **Yíhéyuán (Summer Palace)**

4+4: **fàndiàn** (hotel) **sùshè** (dormitory) **diànhuà** (telephone)

bàogào (report)

zàijiàn (good-bye)

4+4+4: **diànshìjù** (soap opera)

Exercise 4

Read the following words or phrases aloud. Each of them contains a high neutral tone or a low neutral tone. Pay attention to the difference between the high and low neutral tones. Refer to the CD to check your pronunciation.

Low neutral tones:

1. **māma** (mother)
2. **shūshu** (uncle)
3. **gēge** (older brother)
4. **jīnzi** (gold)
5. **xiānsheng** (Mister)
6. **yéye** (grandpa)
7. **bóbo** (uncles)
8. **háizi** (children)
9. **yínzi** (silver)
10. **shénme** (what)
11. **dìdi** (younger brother)
12. **kàn le** (saw)

13. **bàba** (father)
14. **xièxie** (thank you)
15. **mèimei** (younger sister)

High neutral tones:

16. **nǎinai** (grandma)
17. **jiějie** (older sister)

18 **zuǒzhe** (walking)

19. **wǒde** (my, mine)
20. **nǐde** (yours)

Each entry below has an initial sound and a final sound that combine to form complete words. Read the initial and final sounds separately, then read the full word. Check your pronunciation on the audio.

Group A	Group B	Group C
w -àn	**zh -āng**	**ch -én**
j -iāng	**l -ín**	**x -iè**
m -èng	**d -ù**	**f -āng**

day:3

Practice

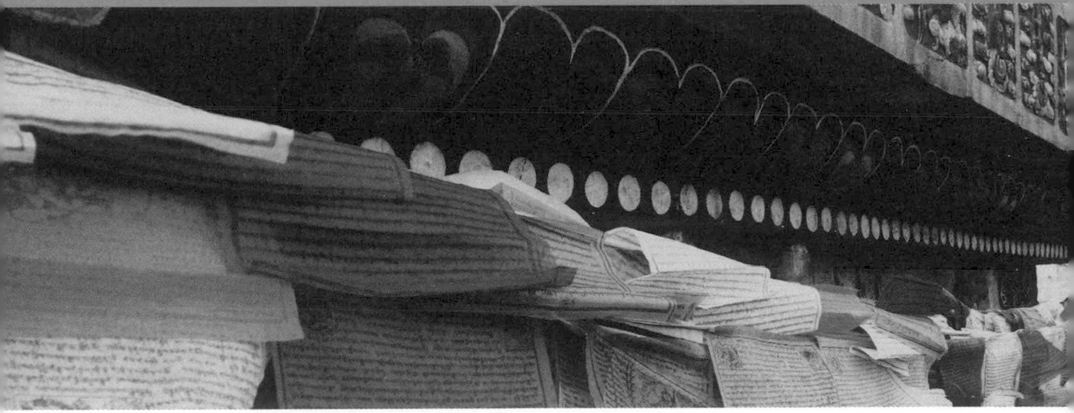

Day 3 is all about practicing what you have learned so far. You will learn the difference between the different sounds of consonants and vowels and semi-vowels and practice writing what you hear. If you need to, go back over the previous lessons to help you with the exercises. You can check your answers at the back of the book.

TV...

Many television programs in China are captioned with Chinese characters. This is because China has many regional dialects, as we saw in Day 2, and their pronunciation can differ so much that they sound like different languages, although note that the written characters are always the same.

Exercises

Exercise 1

Listen to these country names and then write in the country name in Pinyin with tone marks. Pay special attention to the sounds **j, q, x, zh, ch, sh,** and **r**.

1. **China** ....
2. **Hong Kong** ....
3. **Singapore** ....
4. **Sweden** ....
5. **Korea** ....
6. **Japan** ....
7. **Switzerland** ....
8. **Canada** ....
9. **Spain** ....
10. **Scotland** ....

Exercise 2

Listen to these city names, and then put the tone marks over the correct vowel in each word.

1. **Xi'an**
2. **Wuhan**
3. **Nanjing**
4. **Guilin**
5. **Chengdou**
6. **Changchun**
7. **Wulumuqi**

8. **Shenyang**
9. **Shijiazhuang**
10. **Zhengzhou**
11. **Hefei**
12. **Nanchang**
13. **Changsha**
14. **Hangzhou**
15. **Taiyuan**
16. **Fuzhou**
17. **Guangzhou**
18. **Kunming**
19. **Guiyang**
20. **Nanning**
21. **Lanzhou**
22. **Xining**
23. **Lasa** (Lhasa)
24. **Yinchua**
25. **Shenzen**
26. **Suzhou**

Exercise 3

Read aloud the names of the Chinese provinces, paying special attention to the tones.

Refer to the CD to check your pronunciation.

1. **Hébĕi**
2. **Hénán**
4. **Shănxī****
3. **Shānxī***

5. Hēilóngjiāng
6. Jílín
7. Shāndōng
8. Liáoníng
9. Jiāngsū
10. Níngxià
11. Gānsū
12. Qīnghǎi
13. Xīnjiāng
14. Sìchuān
15. Ānhuī
16. Húběi
17. Húnán
18. Zhéjiāng
19. Jiāngxī
20. Guìzhōu
21. Fújiàn
22. Yúnnán
23. Guǎndōng
24. Guǎngxī
25. Xīzàng
26. Nèiménggu
27. Běijīng
28. Shànghǎi
29. Tiājīn
30. Chóngqìng

*sometimes written as "Shanxi" **sometimes written as "Shaanxi"

Exercise 4

Change the following words so that they use the correct spelling of **i**, **u**, and **ü** as semi-vowels at the beginning of a syllable.

1. **īngguó** (England) .... Yīngguó
2. **iángzhōu** (a city) .... Yángzhōu
3. **Mr. Uang** .... Wang
4. **uǒ** (I, me) .... Wo
5. **üènán** (Vietnam) .... Yuenan
6. **iě** (also) .... yě
7. **xüéxí** (to study) .... xuexi
8. **uèi** (hello) .... wei
9. **ī** (one) .... yi
10. **üán** (¥1.00) .... yuan
11. **iǒu** (to have) .... you
12. **īn-iáng** (the two opposing principles in nature) .... yiu yang

Exercise 5

Underline each of the initials in the following words.

1. **Yǒuyì Shāngdiàn** (Friendship Store)
2. **Hǎidiàn** (a district in Beijing)
3. **Gùgōng** (Palace Museum)
4. **Tiānānmén** (Square, Beijing)
5. **Tiāntán** (Temple of Heaven)
6. **Hóngqiáo Shìchǎng** (Pearl Market, Beijing)
7. **Xiùshuǐ Dōngjiē** (Silk Market, Beijing)

8. **Yíhéyuán** (Summer Palace)
9. **Chángchéng** (Great Wall)
10. **Shísānlíng** (Ming Tombs)
11. **dàshǐguǎn** (embassy)
12. **Pānjiāyuán** ("Mud Market," Beijing)

day:4

Numbers

In this section you will learn the numbers in Chinese. You will further practice your pronunciation using rhymes and you will learn how to use the adverb 也 yě meaning too, also.

SUPERSTITIONS...

Many Chinese characters are homophones, and so can be puns that suggest another meaning. For example, the pronunciation of ***sì*** *(four) is similar to* ***sǐ*** *(death), therefore some people avoid the number four. On the other hand, the pronunciation of* ***bā*** *(eight) resembles* ***fā*** *(to become rich), so the number eight is a favorite.*

Vocabulary

New Words I • 生词一

Characters	Pinyin	English
数	**shǔ**	*to count*
数	**shù**	*number*
你	**nǐ**	*you*
也	**yě**	*also*
我	**wǒ**	*I, me*
一	**yī**	*one*
二	**èr**	*two*
三	**sān**	*three*
四	**sì**	*four*
五	**wǔ**	*five*
加	**jiā**	*to add; plus*
六	**liù**	*six*
七	**qī**	*seven*
八	**bā**	*eight*
九	**jiǔ**	*nine*
十	**shí**	*ten*
是	**shì**	*to be (am, is, are, was, were); yes, correct, right*

Counting Rhyme I

你也数，我也数，
Nǐ yě shǔ, wǒ yě shǔ,

一二三四五。
yī, èr, sān, sì, wǔ.

你也加，我也加，
Nǐ yě jiā, wǒ yě jiā,

四五六七八。
sì, wǔ, liù, qī, bā.

九是四加五。
Jiǔ shì sì jiā wǔ.

十是二加八。
Shí shì èr jiā bā

Translation of Counting Rhyme I

You count, and I count, too:

one, two, three, four, five.

You add, and I add, too:

four, five, six, seven, eight.

Nine is four plus five.

Ten is two plus eight.

New Words II • 生词二

Characters	Pinyin	English
一百	**yìbǎi**	*one hundred*
百	**bǎi**	*hundred*
零 (0)	**líng**	*zero*
是不是	**shì búshì**	*Is it?/Are they?*
不是	**búshì**	*No, it is not.*
不	**bù**	*no, not*

千	**qiān**	*thousand*
万	**wàn**	*ten thousand*
亿	**yì**	*billion (hundred million)*

Counting Rhyme II

Here is another counting rhyme. This one lets you practice the difficult sounds "s" and "sh" in the words **sì**, **shí**, and **shì**. When you say **sì**, your tongue is flat and the tip of your tongue touches the lower teeth. When you say **shí** or **shì**, your tongue curls up toward the roof of the mouth, fairly far back. When you say **sìshí**, your tongue is down and then up. But when you say **shísì**, your tongue is up and then down. Good luck!

四是四，
Sì shì sì,

十是十。
Shí shì shí.

十四是十四，
Shísì shì shísì,

四十是四十。
Sìshí shì sìshí.

一百是一零零，是不是？
Yìbǎi shì yī líng líng, shì búshì?

Translation of Counting Rhyme II

Four is four,

Ten is ten.

Fourteen is fourteen,

Forty is forty.

One hundred is one-zero-zero, isn't it?

How many terracotta horses are in this tomb?

Say it in Chinese!

day:5

Counting

Day 5 focuses again on numbers and counting. This time you will focus on the grammatical elements of numbers and how to express them. You will also learn how to use affirmative-negative questions; how to read large numbers and how to use the shì (to be) sentence pattern.

LUCKY NUMBERS…

Chinese people have many lucky associations for numbers, as in "the four kinds of happiness," "the five kinds of luckiness and long life," and "five children reach the summit of achievement."

Grammar

The adverb 也 yě (too, also)

也 yě is an adverb that functions as a conjunction and must come between the subject and the main verb in a sentence.

你也数，我也数 You count, and I count, too.
Nǐ yě shǔ, wǒ yě shǔ.
你也加，我也加 You add, and I also add.
Nǐ yě jiā, wǒ yě jiā.

The 是 shì (to be) sentence pattern

是 shì is a linking verb that usually connects two nouns, indicating that the nouns on either side of 是 are equal or nominative. For example:

九是四加五 Nine is four plus five.
Jiǔ shì sì jiā wǔ.

十是二加八 Ten is two plus eight.
Shí shì èr jiā bā.

Especially when stating numbers, you may reverse the sentence order without any change of meaning.

四加五是九 Four plus five is nine.
Sì jiā wǔshì jiǔ.

二加八是十 Two plus eight is ten.
Èr jiā bā shì shí.

Like all Chinese verbs, 是 shì does not change, no matter what the tense, gender, person, or number is. The negative form of 是 shì is 不是 búshì.

Affirmative-negative questions with 是不是 shì búshì (Is it?/Are they?)

是不是 shì búshì is a question that is formed by combining 是 shì (the positive form) with 不是 búshì (the negative form of 是 shì). This is an "affirmative-negative" question, which can also be called a "yes-or-no" question. The answer to it is either the positive form of 是 shì *(yes)* or its negative form 不是 búshì *(no)*. For example:

Q:

一百是一零零，是不是？ One hundred is one-zero-zero, isn't it?
Yìbǎi shì yī líng líng, shì búshi?

Positive Answer:

是
Shì.

Yes.

Negative Answer:

不是
Búshì.

No.

Any verb can be used in an affirmative-negative question. The answer must be either the affirmative or negative form of the verb in the sentence. For example:

Q:

你数不数数？
Nǐ shǔ bù shǔ shù?

Are you counting the numbers?

Positive Answer:

数
Shǔ .

Yes.

Negative Answer:

不数
Bù shǔ .

No.

Counting to 1000

The numbers 0 to 10:

0	零	**líng**	6	六	**liù**
1	一	**yī**	7	七	**qī**
2	二	**èr**	8	八	**bā**
3	三	**sān**	9	九	**jiǔ**
4	四	**sì**	10	十	**shí**
5	五	**wǔ**			

Say the numbers 0 to 10 aloud.

The numbers 11–19 follow the pattern 十 shí + 1–9:

11	十	+	一	**shíyī**
12	十	+	二	**shí'èr**
13	十	+	三	**shísān**

Say the numbers 11–19 aloud.

The numbers 20–99 follow the pattern 2–9 + 十 shí + 1–9:

21	二	+	十	+	一	**èrshíyī**
34	三	+	十	+	四	**sānshísì**
42	四	+	十	+	二	**sìshí'èr**

Say the numbers 20–99 aloud.

The numbers 101–109 follow the pattern 一百 yìbǎi + 零 líng + 1–9. This is also the pattern for 201–209, 301–309 and so on, all the way up to 901–909:

101	一百	+	零	+	一	**yìbǎi líng yī**
202	二百	+	零	+	二	**èr bǎi líng èr**
303	三百	+	零	+	三	**sān bǎi líng sān**

Say the numbers 101–109 aloud.

If a ten follows a hundred you have to say yìbǎi yīshí (110) (not yìbǎi shí).

110 一百一十 yìbǎi yīshí

The numbers 110–119 follow the pattern 一百 yìbǎi + 一十 yīshí + 一 yī – 十九 shíjiǔ.

111	一百	+	一十	+	一	**yìbǎi yīshí yī**
112	一百	+	一十	+	二	**yìbǎi yīshí'èr**
113	一百	+	一十	+	三	**yìbǎi yīshí sān**
114	一百	+	一十	+	四	**yìbǎi yīshí sì**
115	一百	+	一十	+	五	**yìbǎi yīshí wǔ**
116	一百	+	一十	+	六	**yìbǎi yīshí liù**
117	一百	+	一十	+	七	**yìbǎi yīshí qī**
118	一百	+	一十	+	八	**yìbǎi yīshí bā**
119	一百	+	一十	+	九	**yìbǎi yīshí jiǔ**

Say the numbers 110–119 aloud.

The numbers 120–199 follow the pattern 一百 **yìbǎi** + 2–9 十 **shí** + 1–9:

120	一百	+	二十			**yìbǎi èrshí**
121	一百	+	二十	+	一	**yìbǎi èrshí yī**
122	一百	+	二十	+	二	**yìbǎi èrshí èr**

Count by tens from 120-190, then count from 190-199.

The numbers 210–1,000 follow the pattern 1–9 + 百 **bǎi** + 一十 **yīshí** + 1–9:

212	二	+	百	+	一十	+	二	**èr bǎi yīshí èr**
224	二	+	百	+	二十	+	四	**èr bǎi èrshí sì**
371	三	+	百	+	七十	+	一	**sān bǎi qīshí yī**
537	五	+	百	+	三十	+	七	**wǔ bǎi sānshí qī**
699	六	+	百	+	九十	+	九	**liù bǎi jiǔshí jiǔ**
862	八	+	百	+	六十	+	二	**bā bǎi liùshí èr**
749	七	+	百	+	四十	+	七	**qī bǎi sìshí qī**
999	九	+	百	+	九十	+	九	**jiǔ bǎi jiǔshí jiǔ**
1000	一	+	千					**yìqiān**

Say the example numbers aloud.

Reading large numbers

To read a large number, starting from the left, for each column say the number, followed by the name of that column.

Note: You do not say the name of the units column, **ge**.

For example, 3,895 shown in the illustration below is read as:

sān qiān	**bā bǎi**	**jiǔshí**	**wǔ**
3,	8	9	5
千	百	十	个
qiān	**bǎi**	**shí**	**gè**
1,000s	100s	10s	units

Try this technique with the following numbers:

3,456 9,872 1,030 5,164 8,927

The 是 shì (to be) sentence pattern

To form a sentence in this pattern, replace the subject and predicate in the example with the groups of words given below.

Subject	Verb	Predicate
九 **Jiǔ** Nine	是 **shì** is	四加五 **sì jiā wǔ.** four plus five.
四加五 **sì jiā wǔ**	九 **jiǔ**	

Subject	Verb	Predicate
二加八 **èr jiā bā**		十 **shí**
十 **shí**		二加八 **èr jiā bā**
二加一 **èr jiā yī**		三 **sān**
五加一 **wǔ jiā yī**		六 **liù**
七加四 **qī jiā sì**		十一 **shíyī**
我 **wǒ**		[name]

The affirmative-negative question 是不是 shì búshì

Replace the subject and the predicate in the example with the groups of words given below, then answer the question with either the positive or the negative form of 是 **shì**.

Subject	Affirmative-negative verb	Predicate
一百 **Yìbǎi**	是不是 **shì búshì**	一零零？ **yī líng líng?**

Is one hundred one-zero-zero?

三加五 **Sān jiā wǔ**	八 **bā**
二加二 **Èr jiā èr**	四 **sì**
七加九 **Qī jiā jiǔ**	十六 **shíliù**
二百加三百 **Èr bǎi jiā sān bǎi**	五百 **wǔ bǎi**
你 **Nǐ**	**Lǐ Jiā**

Pronunciation Note: Tone Changes

Remember, **yī** *(one)*, **qī** *(seven)*, **bā** *(eight)*, **bù** *(no)* can each have several different tones.

1. **Yī** can have three different tones.
   A. **Yī** is 1st tone when it is used alone: **yī, èr, sān, sì, wǔ**
   B. **Yī** is 2nd tone when followed by a 4th-tone measure word: **yí kuài** *(one yuan)*
   C. **Yī** is 4th tone when followed by a 1st, 2nd, or 3rd-tone measure word: **yì zhāng** *(one piece)*, **yì máo** *(one mao)*, **yì jiǎo** *(one jiao)*, **yì fēn** *(one fen)*

2. **Qī** and **bā** each can have two tones:

   Qī and **bā** when used alone are 1st tone, but when followed by a 4th-tone measure word, they may change to the 2nd tone:

   qī hào *or* **qí hào** *(the number seven)*

   bā hào *or* **bá hào** *(the number eight)*

3. 不 **bù** (no) is 4th tone, except that when it is followed by a 4th tone word, 不 **bù** changes to 2nd tone:
   不是 **búshì** *(is not)*

Pronunciation Practice

Practice the tone changes of **yī** *(one)*, **qī** *(seven)*, **bā** *(eight)*, and **bù** *(no)*. Read the following phrases aloud and add the tone marks for **yī**, **qī**, **bā**, and **bù** above the appropriate vowels in the chart below. Check your pronunciaton on the CD.

	Pinyin	Characters	English
a.	**1. dìyi**	第一	the number one
	2. yi tiān	一天	one day
	3. yi píng	一瓶	one bottle
	4. yi běn	一本	one copy
	5. yi gè	一个	one piece
	6. yi bēi	一杯	one glass
	7. yi wǎn	一碗	one bowl
	8. yi huà	一划	one stroke
b.	**1. dìqi**	第七	the seventh
	2. qiyuè	七月	July
c.	**1. dìba**	第八	the eighth
	2. bahào	八号	the number eight
d.	**1. bugāo**	不高	not tall
	2. buxíng	不行	not okay
	3. buhǎo	不好	not good
	4. bucuò	不错	not bad
	5. buqù	不去	to not go
	6. buxīn	不新	not new
	7. bubì	不必	not necessary
	8. buzǒu	不走	to not leave

Practice reading aloud the following words with 不 **bù**. Remember that the tone of 不 **bù** changes from 4th to 2nd when followed by a 4th tone. Check your pronunciation on the CD.

Pinyin	Characters	English
1. bù	不	no
2. duìbùqǐ	对不起	I am sorry.
3. bù zhīdào	不知道	I don't know.
4. tīng bùdǒng	听不懂	I can't understand what you said.
5. bù hǎo	不好	not good
6. bù chī	不吃	to not eat
7. bù lái	不来	to not come
8. búyào	不要	to not want
9. búduì	不对	not correct
10. búcuò	不错	good, not bad at all
11. búxiè	不谢	Not at all./You're welcome.
12. búkèqi	不客气	You're welcome.

Read aloud the numbers 0 to 10, organized here by tone.

1st tone	**yī** (1)	**sān** (3)	qī (7)	**bā** (8)
2nd tone	**líng** (0)	**shí** (10)		
3rd tone	**wǔ** (5)	**jiǔ** (9)		
4th tone	**èr** (2)	**sì** (4)	**liù** (6)	

Each entry below has an initial sound and a final sound that combine to form complete words. Read the initial and final sound, then read the full word. Check your pronunciation on the audio.

Group A:		Group B:		Group C:		Group D:	
j	**iē**	**z**	**ū**	**b**	**ō**	**zh**	**ī**
q	**iū**	**c**	**uī**	**p**	**āo**	**ch**	**āi**
x	**iā**	**s**	**ūn**	**m**	**áng**	**sh**	**ān**
				f	**én**	**r**	**ēng**

Read aloud the following words, which have similar sounds.

Group A:

yīshí 一十	**yì shí** 一石	**yímín** 移民
yìmíng 译名	**yī zì** 一字	**yǐzi** 椅子
yì tiān 一天	**yì tián** 易田	

Group B:

èr zǐ 二子	**érzi** 儿子	**èr nǚ** 二女
érnǚ 儿女	**èr duǒ** 二朵	**ěrduo** 耳朵

Group C:

sān rén 三人	**shànrén** 善人	**sān diǎn** 三点
sǎndiǎn 散点	**dàsān** 大三	**dǎsǎn** 打伞

Group D:

sì zhōu 四周	**sīchóu** 丝绸	**sìshū** 四书
sǐshù 死树	**sìshí** 四十	**sīshì** 私事

Group E:

wǔ tiān 五天	**wùtiān** 雾天	**wǔsì** 五四
wúsī 无私	**wǔ huí** 五回	**wùhuì** 误会

Group F:

liùshū 六书	**liǔshù** 柳树	**liù píng** 六瓶
liūbīng 溜冰	**liù jīn** 六斤	**liúxīn** 留心

Group G:

qīshí 七十	**qíshì** 歧视	**qī míng** 七名
qǐmíng 起名	**qī zhé** 七折	**qìchē** 汽车

Group H:

bābā 八八	**bàba** 爸爸	**bāzì** 八字
bǎzi 靶子	**bālù** 八路	**bá shù** 拔树

Group I:

jiǔshí 九十 **jiùshì** 旧事 **jiǔjiǔ** 九九
jiùjiu 舅舅 **jiǔ jīn** 九斤 **jiūxīn** 揪心

Group J:

shí fù 十幅 **shīfu** 师父 **shízì** 十字
shìzi 柿子 **yīshí** 一十 **lìshǐ** 历史

day:6

Counting Exercises

Day 6 puts into practice what you have just learned in Days 4 and 5. You will continue to focus on writing Pinyin and familiarizing yourself with initials and tone marks. Remember to listen to the audio as you go through the exercises to improve your pronunciation and comprehension.

THE CHINESE ABACUS…

The Chinese abacus has been in use for hundreds of years and is a simple device for counting and making mathematical calculations. It was created by Cheng Dawei of the Ming Dynasty.

Using an Abacus

The Chinese abacus has been in use for hundreds of years. There are two beads that each represent five above the bar and five beads that each represent one below the bar.

By simply extending the process that you have already learned for counting, you can read very large numbers. The columns of an abacus from right to left are **gè** *(units)*, **shí** *(tens)*, **bǎi** *(hundreds)*, **qiān** *(thousands)*, **wàn** *(ten thousands)*, **shíwàn** *(hundred thousands)*, **bǎiwàn** *(million)*, **qiānwàn** *(ten million)*, and **yì** *(billion)*.

yì	**qiān**	**bǎi wàn**	**shí wàn**	**wàn**	**qiān**	**bǎi**	**shí**	**gè**
↓	↓	↓	↓	↓	↓	↓	↓	↓
4	7	5,	6	2	3,	4	1	9
亿	千	百	十	万	千	百	十	个
yì	**qiān**	**bǎi**	**shí**	**wàn**	**qiān**	**bǎi**	**shí**	**jiǔ**

This is read **sì-yì qī-qiān wǔ-bǎi liù-shí èr-wàn sān-qiān sì-bǎi yīshí jiǔ**.

Start from the left and say the number and then the name of each column, one by one. Notice that you do not say the **wàn** in **qiānwàn**, **bǎiwàn**, and **shíwàn**. You only need to say **qiān, bǎi, shí, + wàn**.

Exercises

Exercise 1

Listen to the numbers on the CD and then write the correct spelling in Pinyin with tone marks for each number in the blanks below.

1. ....

2. ....

3. ....

4. ....

5. ....

6. ....

7. ....

8. ....

9. ....

10. ....

Exercise 2

Listen to these addition problems and write the answers in Pinyin. First study this vocabulary new word: 几 jĭ (how many/much)

Example:

Question:	二加二是几 **Èr jiā èr shì jĭ?**	How much is two plus two?
Answer:	二加二是四 **Èr jiā èr shì sì.**	Two plus two is four.

1. ....三加六是几？

2. ....十加十是几？

3. ....七加七是几？

4. ....五十加五十是几？

5. ....四十五加六十六是几？

Exercise 3

Listen to these numbers between 11 and 999 and write them as Arabic numerals.

1. ....

2. ....

3. ....

4. ....

5. ....

6. ....

7. ....

8. ....

9. ....

10. ....

Exercise 4

Fill in the initial sound for each Chinese number.

6: .... **iù** **1:** .... **ī**

7: .... **ī** **3:** .... **ān**

8: .... **ā** **5:** .... **ǔ**

9: .... **iǔ** **10:** .... **í**

Exercise 5

Add the following symbols and write the sum as a numeral. Then write the problem and the sum in Pinyin, as in the example.

Example: ◆◆◆◆◆ + ◆◆◆ = 8 **Wǔ jiā sān shì bā.**

1. ◆◆◆◆ + ◆◆◆◆◆ = ...

2. ◆◆◆◆◆◆◆ + ◆◆◆◆◆◆◆ = ...

3. ◆◆◆◆ + ◆◆◆◆ = ...

4. ◆◆◆ + ◆◆◆◆◆◆◆◆ = ...

5. ◆◆◆◆◆◆ + ◆◆◆◆◆◆◆ = ...

6. ◆◆◆◆◆ + ◆◆◆◆◆◆ = ...

7. ◆◆◆◆◆ + ◆◆ = ...

Traditional Complex Forms of Numbers

You will notice that Chinese coins and currency have numbers written in the traditional, complex form instead of the modern, simplified form that you have been learning. The complex forms are used in banking (including on checks, payment orders, and receipts) to avoid the problem of someone easily altering 一 **yī** *(one)* to 十 **shí** *(ten)* or 千 **qiān** *(thousand)*. Here are the traditional, complex forms of the numbers:

壹 **1** 貳 **2** 叁 **3** 肆 **4** 伍 **5** 陸 **6**

柒 **7** 捌 **8** 玖 **9** 拾 **10** 佰 **100** 仟 **1000**

day: 7

Money

Day 7 continues on the numbers theme. Here you will learn the vocabulary you need to discuss money and hear some simple dialogues to increase your understanding of Mandarin.

EXCHANGE IN CHINA...

Foreign currency can be exchanged at most major banks, international airports, some large hotels, some large department stores, and some tourist areas. You need to show your passport or a foreign resident's ID. Be sure to keep the receipt when you exchange money because you will need those receipts in order to convert RMB back to foreign currency. It is illegal to exchange foreign currency on the street, and you are likely to be given counterfeit money if you do. Foreign credit cards can also be used to obtain RMB from Chinese ATMs but you can expect to pay a fee for the transaction.

Vocabulary

请问，在哪儿换钱？ **Qǐng wèn, zài nǎr huànqián?**	*Where can I exchange money?*
这个多少钱？ **Zhè ge duōshao qián?**	*How much is this?*

New Words I • 生词一

Characters	Pinyin	English
你好	**nǐ haǒ**	*Hello! How do you do!*
小姐	**xiǎojie**	*Miss, Ms., young lady (used to address female workers in banks, restaurants, stores, hotels, etc.)*
小	**xiǎo**	*little, small, young*
这个	**zhè ge/zhèi ge**	*this one, this*
这	**zhè/zhèi**	*this*
个	**gè/ge**	*(measure word for people or things)*
多少	**duōshao**	*How many?, How much?*
钱	**qián**	*money*
块	**kuài**	*¥1.00 (colloquial form of* 元 **yuán***), dollar*
毛	**máo**	*¥0.10 (colloquial form of* 角 **jiǎo***); a surname*
那个	**nà ge/nèi ge**	*that one*
那	**nà/nèi**	*that*
呢	**ne**	*How about (you, this, that)?*
两	**liǎng**	*two*
要	**yào**	*to want, would like, need*
收	**shōu**	*to accept, to receive*
美圆	**Měiyuán**	*U.S. currency, dollar*

圆	**yuán**	*¥1.00 (formal written form of* 元 **yuán***), dollar*
请	**qǐng**	*please; to invite*
问	**wèn**	*to ask*
请问	**qǐngwèn**	*May I ask? (Used before asking a question to someone you don't know.)*
在	**zài**	*in, at; to be in, to be at, to exist*
哪儿	**nǎr**	*Where? (Northern China)*
哪	**nǎ**	*Which? What?*
换	**huàn**	*to exchange*
人民币	**Rénmínbì**	*People's currency (RMB, ¥)*
人民	**rénmín**	*people*
币	**bì**	*currency, money, coin*
中国银行	**Zhōngguó Yínháng**	*Bank of China*
中国	**Zhōngguó**	*China*
银行	**yínháng**	*bank*
谢谢	**xièxie**	*thank you*
不谢	**búxiè**	*not at all, you're welcome*

Dialogue I • 对话一

Roles

A:	Foreigner in China	外国人 **wàiguórén;**
B:	Chinese saleswoman	小姐 **xiǎojie**

A:	你好！小姐，这个多少钱？	**Nǐ hǎo! Xiǎojie, zhège duōshao qián?**
B:	这个一百四十块三毛八。	**Zhèi ge yìbǎi sìshí kuài sān máo bā.**
A:	那个呢？	**Nèi ge ne?**
B:	那个是一百零八块两毛五。	**Nèi ge shì yìbǎi líng bā kuài liǎng máo wǔ.**
A:	我要这个。	**Wǒ yào zhèi ge.**
B:	不收美圆。	**Bù shōu Měiyuán.**
A:	请问，在哪儿换人民币？	**Qǐngwèn, zài nǎr huàn Rénmínbì?**
B:	在中国银行。	**Zài Zhōngguó Yínháng.**
A:	谢谢。	**Xièxie.**
B:	不谢。	**Búxiè.**

Translation of Dialogue I

A: Miss, how much is this?
B: This is 140 kuai, three mao, and eight (fen).
A: How about that one?
B: That one is 108 kuai, two mao, and five (fen).
A: I want this one.
B: I don't accept U.S. dollars.
A: May I ask, where can I exchange for Renminbi?
B: At the Bank of China.
A: Thank you.
B: You're welcome.

The first sentence spoken by the saleswoman is a short form that omits 分 **fēn** at the end of the sentence. The name of the last (smallest) unit of money may be dropped when an amount of money is not a round number. Here is another example:

十块五毛三 **shí kuài wǔ máo sān**	¥10.53

Its long form would be:

十块五毛三分 **shí kuài wǔ máo sān fēn**	¥10.53;

an even longer form would be:

十块五毛三分钱 **shí kuài wǔ máo sān fēn qián**	¥10.53.

New Words II • 生词二

Characters	Pinyin	English
好	**hǎo**	*good, well, OK*
元	**yuán**	*¥1.00, dollar*
角	**jiǎo**	*¥0.10*
分	**fēn**	*¥0.01, cent*
外国人	**wàiguórén**	*foreigner*
美国人	**Měiguórén**	*American (person)*
港币	**Gǎngbì**	*Hong Kong dollar (HK$)*
外币	**wàibì**	*foreign currency*
这儿	**zhèr**	*here*
那儿	**nàr**	*there*
兑换单	**duìhuàndān**	*exchange form*
签字	**qiānzì**	*to sign, to affix a signature*

Dialogue II • 对话二

Roles

A:	American	美国人 **Měiguórén;**
B:	Bank clerk/teller	小姐 **xiǎojie**

A:	你好! 小姐,我换人民币。	**Nǐ hǎo! Xiǎojie, wǒ huàn Rénmínbì.**
B:	你好! 请问你换多少钱?	**Nǐ hǎo! Qǐng wèn nǐ huàn duōshao qián?**
A:	我换一百美圆。	**Wǒ huàn yìbǎi Měiyuán.**
B:	好。	**Hǎo.**
A:	这是多少人民币?	**Zhè shì duōshao Rénmínbì?**
B:	这是八百二十元两角六分。	**Zhè shì bā bǎi èrshí yuán liǎng jiǎo liù fēn.**
A:	谢谢。	**Xièxie.**
B:	不谢。	**Búxiè.**

Translation of Dialogue II

A: How do you do! Miss, I want to exchange for Renminbi.
B: How do you do! May I ask, how much do you want to exchange?
A: I want to exchange 100 dollars.
B: OK.
A: How much is this in Renminbi?
B: This is 820 yuan, two jiao, and six fen.
A: Thank you.
B: You're welcome.

day:8

Asking Questions

Day 8 teaches you question words focused around exchanging money and everyday useful phrases. You will learn the essential grammatical forms needed to ask and answer questions. Don't forget to listen along to the CD for your pronunciation practice.

LUCKY NUMBERS...

The numbers ***èr bā*** *(two eight) indicate "two sides become rich." Therefore, in the business world, numbers such as 28; 28,000; 88 and 888 are favorites. In Hong Kong an automobile license plate with the number "888" can be sold for a high price.*

Grammar

The question word 呢 ne (how about, what about, where is)

呢 **ne** is a modal particle that is used at the end of a sentence. Here it is used to make a question:

那个呢？ **Nà ge ne?**	How about that one?
小姐呢？ **Xiǎojie ne?**	Where is the saleswoman?

The question word 多少 duōshao (how many, how much)

多少 duōshao usually comes after the verb. Notice that this is unlike the word order of English. An exception is when 多少 **duōshao** forms an independent sentence such as 多少钱？**Duōshao qián?** *(How much money?)* or 多少人？**Duōshao rén?** *(How many people?)*.

Q:	这是多少钱？ **Zhè shì duōshao qián?**	How much is this?
A:	这是一百美圆。 **Zhè shì yìbǎi Měiyuán.**	This is 100 dollars.

二 èr (two) and 两 liǎng (two)

Both 两 **liǎng** and 二 **èr** mean two, but they have different uses:

a. 两 **liǎng** is the quantity two (a cardinal number)

两个人	**liǎng ge rén**	two people
两块钱	**liǎng kuài qián**	two kuài
两层楼	**liǎng céng lóu**	two floors
两瓶啤酒	**liǎng píng píjiǔ**	two bottles of beer
两个门	**liǎng ge mén**	two doors

b. 二 **èr** is for the second in a sequence (an ordinal number)

二层	**èrcéng**	second floor
二楼	**èrlóu**	second floor; second building
二门	**èrmén**	second door

二号	**èrhào**	second day of the month; number two
二班	**èrbān**	second group

There are a few words that may use either **liǎng** or **èr**:

Two kilos, which is a quantity, may be either 两斤 **liǎng jīn** or 二斤 **èr jīn**.

*Two **máo***, which is a quantity, may be either 两毛 **liǎng máo** or 二毛 **èr máo**.

c. The number 2 is 二 **èr** (not 两 **liǎng**) in 12, 20–29, 32, 42 up to 92 and 102, 202, etc.

d. When the number 2 is in 200, 2,000, 20,000, etc., you may use either 两 **liǎng** or 二 **èr**. The northern and the southern Chinese have different preferences. For example:

	Northern	*Southern*
200	两百 **liǎng bǎi**	二百 **èr bǎi**
2,000	两千 **liǎng qiān**	二千 **èr qiān**
20,000	两万 **liǎng wàn**	二万 **èr wàn**

在 zài (be in/at) + place name

在 **zài** as a preposition *(in, at)* is always followed by a place word to form a prepositional phrase and means to be in or at some place.

在哪儿换钱？ (At) where (can I) exchange money?
Zài nǎr huànqián?
在银行换钱。 (You can) exchange money at the bank.
Zài yínháng huànqián.

In Chinese the "**zài** + place" prepositional phrase must always come before the verb:

Subject + **zài** + place + verb + object

我在银行换钱。 I exchange money at the bank.
Wǒ zài yínháng huànqián.

Notice that the Chinese word order is different from English, which can have *"in the bank"* at the end of the sentence.

The question word 哪儿 nǎr (where)

哪儿 **nǎr** is an interrogative pronoun that is often used with the preposition 在 **zài** *(in, at)* to ask questions. When you ask the question *Where is . . .?*, the pattern is:

在 **zài** + 哪儿 **nǎr** + Verb + Object

在	哪儿	换	钱？	Where can I exchange money?
Zài	**nǎr**	**huàn**	**qián?**	

Units of money

Review the formal and colloquial terminology for money. Remember to be consistent in using either the formal or the colloquial usage, without mixing them.

	Units	Tenths	Hundredths
Formal Usage	元 **yuán**	角 **jiǎo**	分 **fēn**
Colloquial Usage	块 **kuài**	毛 **máo**	分 **fēn**

The following chart shows some examples of how to say an amount of money. Just insert the number before the name of its unit. For example:

	Formal			Colloquial		
¥1.32	**1**元 **yì yuán**	**3** 角 **sān jiǎo**	**2** 分 **èr fēn**	**1** 块 **yí kuài**	**3** 毛 **sān máo**	2 **èr**
¥4.55	**4**元 **sì yuán**	**5**角 **wǔ jiǎo**	**5**分 **wǔ fēn**	**4**块 **sì kuài**	**5**毛 **wǔ máo**	**5** **wǔ**

	Formal		Colloquial	
¥6.70	**6**元 **liù yuán**	**7**角 **qī jiǎo**	**6**块 **liù kuài**	**7** **qī**
¥189.00	**189**元 **yìbǎi bāshí jiǔ yuán**		**189**块 **yìbǎi bāshíjiǔ kuài**	

Asking questions with 多少 duōshao

Practice using 多少 **duōshao**, *how many/how much*, to form questions. Fill in the chart below using the subjects and objects provided. The first one is done for you.

Question				Answer			
Subject	*Verb*	*Int.*	*Object*	*Subject*	*Verb*	*No.*	*Object*
这 **Zhè**	是 **shì**	多少 **duōshao**	钱？ **qián?**	这 **Zhè**	是 **shì**	一百 **yìbǎi**	美元。 **Měiyuán.**
How much money is this?				This is $100.			
那 **nà**	**duōshao**	人民币 **Rénmínbì**	那 **nà**		**shì**	**300**	**RMB**
这 **zhè**			美元 **Měiyuán**	这 **zhè**		**150**	**US$**
那 **nà**			港币 **(HK$)** **Gǎngbì**	那 **nà**		**500**	**HK$**
这 **zhè**			块 **kuài**	这 **zhè**		**1,000**	块 **kuài**
那 **nà**			元 **yuán**	那 **nà**		**95**	元 **yuán**
这 **zhè**			钱 **qián**	这 **zhè**		**200**	块钱 **kuài qián**

Asking questions with 呢 ne

Form a question by adding 呢 **ne** at the end of a sentence.

Subject	Verb	Object	Subject	Particle
这 **Zhè**	是 **shì**	一百块， **yìbǎi kuài,**	那个 **nà ge**	呢？ **ne?**
This is 100 kuai, how about that one?				
Practice this using the subjects, verbs and objects provided.				
我 **wǒ**		[your name]	你 **nǐ**	
我 **wǒ**		美国人 **Měiguórén**	你 **nǐ**	

我 **wǒ**		要 **yào**	这个 **zhè ge**	你 **nǐ**
我 **wǒ**	换	钱 **huàn**	你 **qián nǐ**	

The number two

Practice the number two. When two precedes a measure word, use 两 **liǎng** (not 二 **èr**).

Number	Measure word	Noun
两 **Liǎng**	块 **kuài**	钱。 **qián.**
	角 **jiǎo**	人民币 **Rénmínbì**
	百 **bǎi**	港币 **Gǎngbì**
	分 **fēn**	钱 **qián**
	美元 **Měiyuán**	

Where?

Use the pattern "**zài** + **nǎr** + Verb + Object" to ask *Where is. . .?*

Question				Answer	
Qǐngwèn	**zài + nǎr**	**Verb**	**Object**	**Zài**	Location
请问 **Qǐng wèn**	在哪儿 **zài nǎr**	换 **huàn**	钱？ **qián?**	在 **Zài**	中国银行。 **Zhōngguó Yínháng.**
May I ask, where can I exchange money?				At the Bank of China.	
			美元 **Měiyuán**		这儿 **zhèr**
			人民币 **Rénmínbì**		那儿 **nàr**
			港币 **Gǎngbì**		中国银行 **Zhōngguó Yínháng**

Pronunciation Note: Tone Changes: 3+3→2+3

Whenever a 3rd tone is followed by another 3rd tone, the first one changes to a 2nd tone. For example:

wǔ jiǎo 五角	→	**wú jiǎo**	five jiao
xǐzǎo 洗澡	→	**xízǎo**	to take a bath
shěngzhǎng 省长	→	**shéngzhǎng**	provincial governor
zǒngtǒng 总统	→	**zóngtǒng**	a nation's president

When three or more 3rd tones are in succession, all except the last one change to 2nd tones. For example:

Wǒ hěn hǎo. 我很好。	→	**Wó hén hǎo.**	I am very well.
Wǒ yě hěn hǎo. 我也很好。	→	**Wó yé hén hǎo.**	I am very well, too.

Pronunciation Practice

Read the following numbers and words aloud, paying special attention to the tone combinations in each.

Pinyin	Characters	English
1. **Nǐ hǎo!**	你好!	Hello!
2. **hěn hǎo**	很好	very good
3. **Běihǎi**	北海	the North Sea
4. **bǔkǎo**	补考	make-up test
5. **hǎidǎo**	海岛	island
6. **shuǐjiǎo**	水饺	dumpling
7. **xiǎojie**	小姐	Miss
8. **bǎoxiǎn**	保险	insurance
9. **lǎoshǔ**	老鼠	mouse
10. **zuǒshǒu**	左手	left hand
11. **qǐdǎo**	祈祷	to pray
12. **lǎohǔ**	老虎	tiger

13. qǐngtiē	请贴	invitation
14. Wǒ xiǎng xǐzǎo	我想洗澡。	I want to take a bath
15. zǒngtǒngfǔ	总统俯	the office building of the president

Read the following numbers and words aloud in Chinese, paying special attention to the tone combinations in each. Check your pronunciation on the CD.

1. 1999

2. 1959

3. 1995

4. 9595

6. 6845

7. 9059

8. 3737

9. 2000

10. 2001

11. cèsuǒ

12. Xīmén

13. sìjiào

14. sháoyuán

15. qīhàolóu

Each entry below has an initial sound and a final sound that combine to form complete words. Read the initial sound and the final sound, then read the full word. Check your pronunciation on the CD.

Group A:		Group B:		Group C:		Group D:	
g	**uàn**	j	**iāng**	d	**é**	b	**ǎng**
k	**àn**	q	īng	t	**ái**	p	**ěng**
h	**ào**	x	**uān**	l	**iáo**	m	**ěi**
				n	**ú**	f	**ǎn**

Read the following numbers and words aloud in Chinese, paying special attention to the tone combinations in each. Check your pronunciation on the CD.

1. **Niǔyuē** (New York)
2. **Wōtàihuá** (Ottawa)
3. **Bōshìdùn** (Boston)
4. **Mèngfēisī** (Memphis)
5. **Luòshānjī** (Los Angeles)
6. **Jiùjīnshān** (San Francisco)
7. **Fèichéng** (Philadelphia)
8. **Huáshèngdùn** (Washington, D.C.)
9. **Bālí** (Paris)
10. **Lúndūn** (London)
11. **Wéiyěnà** (Vienna)
12. **Bólín** (Berlin)
13. **Āmǔsītèdān** (Amsterdam)
14. **Huìlíndùn** (Wellington)

day:9

Exercises

Day 9 finalises the money theme. Here you will practice what you have learned in the last two lessons and further work on your comprehension and listening skills. You will also learn about Chinese superstitions.

LUCKY FOR SOME...

Another lucky number is nine. It is an ultimate number in ***yin-yang*** *philosophy because when* ***yin*** *or* ***yang*** *reaches the value of nine, any further increase will bring it to ten, where* ***yin*** *turns into* ***yang*** *and where* ***yang*** *turns into* ***yin****. Therefore nine represents completeness or fullness in Chinese culture. As such, nine dragons are a sign of the emperor and some people use nine in their names.*

Exercises

Exercise 1

Read and listen to the following dialogue and then answer the questions:

A: Foreigner 外国人 **wàiguórén**;

B: Bank clerk 小姐 **xiǎojie**;

A: 小姐，我要换钱。

B: 你要换多少？

A: 我要换两百美圆的人民币。

B: 好。

A: 这是两百美圆。

B: 这是一千六百六十块人民币。

A: 谢谢。

B: 不谢。再见。

A: 再见。

Questions:

1. What did the foreigner want to do? ....

....

....

2. What kind of currency and what amount did he want to exchange at the bank? ......

....

....

3. What amount did he receive?..

....

....

4. **How many RMB equal one U.S. dollar?** ....

....

....

Exercise 2

Read and listen to the dialogue and then answer the questions.

A: Foreigner 外国人 **wàiguórén**;

B: Bank clerk 小姐 **xiǎojie**;

A: 小姐，这个多少钱？

B: 这个两百块。

A: 那个呢？

B: 那个两块五。

A: 我要那个。

B: 好。

A: 谢谢！

B: 不谢。再见。

A: 再见。

Questions:

1. **Which item did the American want?** ....

....

....

2. **How much did he pay the clerk?** ....

....

....

....

3. What did the clerk say after he gave her the money? ....

....

....

....

Exercise 3

All the words for RMB units of money are measure words. Practice using 两 **liǎng**, *two*, with the units of money given. Write them in Pinyin and read them aloud.

1. ¥2.00 块 ....

2. ¥0.02 分 ....

3. ¥222.00 元 ....

4. ¥2000 千 ....

5. ¥2.20 毛 ....

6. ¥200 百 ....

7. ¥0.20 角 ....

8. $2.00 美元 ....

Exercise 4

Write the following numbers in Pinyin and read them aloud.

37 ....

56 ....

94 ....

27 ....

19 ....

65 ....

12 ....

73 ....

100 ....

109 ....

123 ....

176 ....

day: 10

Café Culture

Day 10 introduces you to café culture and the vocabulary you will need to order from the menu and ask questions. You will also learn how to address wait staff politely. Listen to the dialogues for typical conversations in this environment.

WAITER!

服务员 ***fúwùyuán*** *is the general term for waiters and waitresses. However a waiter is usually referred to as* 师傅 ***shīfu*** *and a waitress as* 小姐 ***xiǎojie****. But be alert for regional usage—in some places, especially in the south,* 小姐 ***xiǎojie*** *has a slang meaning of "call girl," and the term for a waitress is* 小妹 ***xiǎomèi*** *("little sister").*

Vocabulary

Key Expressions

您要什么菜？ *What dishes would you like to order to order?*
Nín yào shénme cài?

我要这个菜。 *I want this dish.*
Wǒ yào zhè ge cài.

我还要酸辣汤。 *I also want hot-and-sour soup.*
Wǒ hái yào suān làtāng.

这是牛肉吗？ *Is this beef?*
Zhè shì niúròu ma?

不要了，谢谢！ *I don't want any more, thank you!*
Bú yào le, xièxie.

New Words 1 • 生词一

Characters	Pinyin	English
食堂	**shítáng**	*cafeteria*
吃饭	**chīfàn**	*to eat a meal*
吃	**chī**	*to eat*
饭	**fàn**	*meal; cooked rice*
吗	**ma**	(forms a question)
很	**hěn**	*very, very much*
您	**nín**	*you* (polite form)
什么	**shénme**	*What?*
菜	**cài**	*dish, vegetable*
牛肉	**niúròu**	*beef*
牛	**niú**	*cow*

肉	**ròu**	*meat* (When combined with the word for an animal, means a specific type of meat. When used alone, often implies "pork".)
猪肉	**zhūròu**	*pork*
猪	**zhū**	*pig*
米饭	**mǐfàn**	*cooked rice*
馒头	**mántou**	*steamed bread, steamed bun*
还	**hái**	*in addition, still, yet*
了	**le**	(indicates a change of situation or completed action)

Dialogue I • 对话一

Roles

A:	Customer	顾客 **gùkè**;
B:	Server	服务员 **fúwùyuán**

A:	你好吗？	**Nǐ hǎo ma?**
B:	我很好，您呢？	**Wǒ hěn hǎo, nín ne?**
A:	我也很好。	**Wǒ yě hěn hǎo.**
B:	您要什么菜？	**Nín yào shénme cài ?**
A:	我要这个菜。这个菜是牛肉吗？	**Wǒ yào zhè ge cài. Zhè ge cài shì niúròu ma?**
B:	不是，是猪肉。那个是牛肉。	**Búshì, shì zhūròu. Nà ge shì niúròu.**
A:	我要那个菜。	**Wǒ yào nà ge cài.**
B:	您要米饭吗？	**Nín yào mǐfàn ma?**
A:	不要，我要馒头。	**Bú yào, wǒ yào mántou.**
B:	还要什么？	**Hái yào shénme?**
A:	不要了。谢谢!	**Bú yào le. Xièxie!**
B:	不谢!	**Búxiè!**

Translation of Dialogue I

A: How are you?
B: I am fine, and you?

A: I am also fine.
B: What [dishes] would you like to order?
A: I want this one. Is it beef?
B: No, it is pork. That one is beef.
A: I'll have that dish.
B: Would you like rice?
A: No, I would like steamed bread.
B: Anything else?
A: No, thank you.
B: You're welcome.

New Words II • 生词二

Characters	Pinyin	English
你们	**nǐmen**	*you* (plural)
有	**yǒu**	*to have*
鸡	**jī**	*chicken*
鱼	**yú**	*fish*
都	**dōu**	*all,* both Adverb: never used to describe a noun
汤	**tāng**	*soup*
鸡蛋汤	**jīdàntāng**	*egg-drop soup*
鸡蛋	**jīdàn**	*egg*
和	**hé**	*and*
酸辣汤	**suānlàtāng**	*hot-and-sour soup*
酸	**suān**	*sour*
辣	**là**	*spicy, hot*

面条	**miàntiáo**	*noodles*
饼	**bǐng**	*fried bread*

Dialogue II • 对话二

Roles

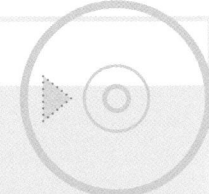

A:	Customer	顾客 **gùkè**;
B:	Server	服务员 **fúwùyuán**

A:	请问，你们有什么菜？	**Qǐng wèn, nǐmen yǒu shénme cài?**
B:	鸡，鱼，肉都有。	**Jī, yú, ròu dōu yǒu.**
A:	我要一个鸡，一个鱼。	**Wǒ yào yí ge jī, yí ge yú.**
B:	要不要汤？	**Yào búyào tāng?**
A:	你们有什么汤？	**Nǐmen yǒu shénme tāng?**
B:	鸡蛋汤和酸辣汤。	**Jīdàntāng hé suānlàtāng.**
A:	要一个鸡蛋汤。	**Yào yí ge jīdàntāng.**
B:	还要什么？	**Hái yào shénme?**
A:	还要一个面条，一个饼。谢谢!	**Hái yào yí ge miàntiáo, yí ge bǐng. Xièxie!**
B:	不谢。	**Búxiè.**

Translation of Dialogue II

A: May I ask, what dishes do you have?
B: Chicken, fish, and meat (dishes): we have all of them.
A: I want one chicken dish and one fish (dish).
B: Would you like soup?
A: What kinds of soup do you have?
B: We have egg-drop soup and hot-and-sour soup.
A: I'd like an egg-drop soup.
B: Anything else?
A: I also want one (order of) noodles and one (order of) fried bread. Thank you.
B: Not at all.

day: 11

Cafeterias

In Day 11 you will learn the grammar you need when eating out. You will learn to use the particle *le* and how to say you want more, as well as practice your pronunciation.

SHÍTÁNG 食堂 (CAFETERIA)

Almost all work places in China have a 食堂 ***shítáng****, which is a cafeteria or dining hall, including a "faculty cafeteria" (教师食堂 jiàoshī shítáng) at schools or an "employee cafeteria" (职工食堂* ***zhígōng shítáng****) at government agencies, companies, and other places of work. The word 食堂* ***shítáng*** *usually indicates self-service eateries. Coupons or vouchers are often used instead of cash. Chinese colleges usually have a separate foreigners' cafeteria called 留学生食堂* ***liúxuéshēng shítáng****. Foreigners are expected to eat in these and not at the regular cafeteria for Chinese people. These cafeterias usually sell both Chinese-style food and Western-style food.*

Grammar

The question word 吗 ma

吗 **ma** is added to the end of an affirmative sentence to make a yes-or-no question. It is the most commonly used form of question in Chinese. 吗 **ma** is always a neutral tone.

这个菜是牛肉吗？ Is this dish a beef dish?
Zhè ge cài shì niúròu ma?

The question word 什么 shénme (what)

什么 **shénme** is an adverb that functions as a conjunction and must come between the subject and the main verb in a sentence.

您要什么 What do you want?/What would you like to order?
Nín yào shénme?

什么 **shénme** can also be put at the beginning of a sentence:

什么是"牛肉"？ What is "niúròu"?
Shénme shì "niúròu"?

The particle 了 le

了 **le** is an important particle in Chinese, and it has several functions. 了 **le** in the previous dialogues serves two functions, which can occur separately or simultaneously:

1. In Chinese, an action or event has an "aspect," independent of whether it occurs in the past, present, or future. The "aspect" of an action or event is its current situation, such as "in progress" or "completed". 了 **le** following a verb indicates the action is completed or the event is concluded. Notice that 了 **le**, as an aspect particle, does not indicate past or present tense, even though "verb + 了 **le**" often refers to an action that took place in the past.

2. 了 **le** at the end of a sentence indicates a change of situation or that a new situation has occurred. An example from dialogue 1 in lesson 10 is "不要了 **búyào le** *No thank you* (Meaning *"I don't want to order any more."*)

了 **le** can occur after the verb and also at the end of the sentence, serving both functions together. It shows that the action associated with *"I want"* is completed and that *"I don't want any more"* is a new situation.

(In a negative sentence these functions are accomplished by using a negative adverb 没 **méi** or 没有 **méiyǒu** before the verb. 了 **le** is not used.)

我吃了。 I have eaten. [the action of eating is over]
Wǒ chī le.
我没(有)吃。 I haven't eaten.
Wǒ méi (yǒu) chī.

The adverb 都 dōu in a topic-comment sentence

鸡，鱼，肉都有 **Jī, yú, ròu dōu yǒu** (Chicken, fish, and meat: we have all of them).

In this sentence, the topic is 鸡，鱼，肉 **jī, yú, ròu**, and the comment is 都有 **dōu yǒu**. The real subject, 我们 **wǒmen** *(we)*, is skipped. The topic-comment structure is a very common sentence pattern in Chinese.

Affirmative-negative questions (with any verb)

You have already seen the affirmative-negative question with 是不是 **shì búshì** *(yes or no?)*. Affirmative-negative questions can be formed with any verb. 要不要 **yào búyào** *(do you want)* is an affirmative-negative question formed by combining the positive form of the verb (要 **yào**) with the negative form of the verb (不要 **búyào**). The answer is simply either the positive or the negative form of the verb. For example:

Q: 你要 不要 米饭？ Do you want rice?
Nǐ yào búyào mǐfàn?

A: 要。 Yes. *or* 不要。 No.
Yào. **Búyào.**

The particle 吗 ma

The particle 吗 **ma** is used at the end of a sentence to turn a statement into a question.

Subject	Verb/Adj	Object	ma
这个菜	是	牛肉	吗？
Zhè ge cài shì	**niúròu**		**ma?**

Is this a beef dish?

Practice asking questions with the question word 吗 **ma** and the subjects, verbs and objects below.

那 **Nà**	猪肉 **zhūròu**	
你 **Nǐ**	要 **yào**	鸡蛋汤 **jīdàntāng**
你们 **Nǐmen**	有 **yǒu**	馒头 **mántou**
你 **Nǐ**	换 **huàn**	钱 **qián**
你 **Nǐ**	好 **hǎo**	
那个菜 **Zhè ge cài**	辣 **là**	

The question word 什么 shénme (what)

A. Practice making new sentences with 什么 **shénme**:

Question			Answer		
Subject	*Verb*	*Int.*	*Subject*	*Verb*	*Object*
您 **Nín**	要 **yào**	什么？ **shénme?**	我 **Wǒ**	要 **yào**	牛肉。 **niúròu.**
What would you like to order?			I want beef.		
	吃 **chī**				面条 **miàntiáo**
	吃 **chī**				面条 **miàntiáo**
	有 **yǒu**			有 **yǒu**	鸡和鱼 **jī hé yú**
	还要 **hái yào**			还要 **hái yào**	米饭 **mǐfàn**
	有 **yǒu**	什么汤 **shénme tāng**		有 **yǒu**	酸辣汤 **suānlàtāng**
	换 **huàn**	什么钱 **shénme qián**		换 **huàn**	美元 **Měiyuán**

B. Now practice asking questions with 什么 **shénme** at the beginning of a sentence:

Question			Answer		
Subject	*Verb*	*Object*	*Subject*	*Verb*	*Object*
什么 **Shénme** What is "niúròu"?	是 **shì**	"牛肉"？ **"niúròu"?**	"牛肉" **"Niúròu"** "Niúròu" is beef.	**shì**	是 **beef.** **beef.**
		馒头 **mántou**	馒头 **mántou**		steamed bread
		饼 **bǐng**	饼 **bǐng**		fried bread
		面条 **miàntiáo**	面条 **miàntiáo**		noodles
		人民币 **Rénmínbì**	人民币 **Rénmínbì**		中国钱 **Zhōngguó qián**
		一元 **yì yuán**	一元 **yì yuán**		十个角 **shí ge jiǎo**
		港币 **Gǎngbì**	港币 **Gǎngbì**		HK$

The particle 了 le

The particle 了 **le** at the end of a sentence or after a verb indicates the "aspect" of an action that is completed. To answer a question with 了 **le**, use the pattern "不 **bú** … 了 **le**" *(not … any more)* which indicates a change of situation.

Practice asking questions with the question word 吗 **ma** and answering with 了 **le**:

Question				Answer		
Subject	**hái** + *verb*	*Object*	**ma**	*Negative of Verb* + **le**		
你 **Nǐ** Would you like	还要 **hái yào**	菜 **cài** more dishes?	吗？ **ma?**	不 **Bú** (I) don't want any more.	要 **yào**	了。 **le.**
	还吃 **hái chī**	米饭 **mǐfàn**			吃 **chī**	
	还要 **hái yào**	这个菜 **zhè ge cài**			要 **yào**	

还吃	鱼	吃
hái chī	**yú**	**chī**
还要	汤	要
hái yào	**tāng**	**yào**
还吃	面条	吃
hái chī	**miàntiáo**	**chī**

Affirmative-negative questions

An affirmative-negative question can be formed with any verb. Practice asking questions with this pattern and answering in both the affirmative and the negative.

Question		Answer
Verb in Affirmative/ Negative	*Object*	*Affirmative Answer/ Negative Answer*
要不要	这个菜？	要。/不要。
Yào búyào	**zhè ge cài?**	**Yào./Búyào.**
Would you like this dish?		Yes, I would./No, I wouldn't.
	米饭	要馒头/不要米饭
	mǐfàn	**Yào mántou./Búyào mǐfàn.**
	这个菜	要那个菜/不要这个菜
	zhè ge cài	**Yào nà ge cài./Búyào zhè ge cài.**
	汤	要菜/不要汤
	tāng	**Yào cài./Búyào tāng.**
	面条	要饼/不要面条
	miàntiáo	**Yào bǐng./Búyào miàntiáo.**
	猪肉	要牛肉/不要猪肉
	zhūròu	**Yào niúròu./Búyào zhūròu.**
	鱼	要鸡/不要鱼
	yú	**Yào jī./Búyào yú.**

Questions with 还要 hái yào (to still want, to want more)

Use the following words to make new sentences with this pattern.

Question				Answer	
Subject	**hái** + *verb*	*Object*	**ma**	**Hái** + *verb*	*Object*
你 **Nǐ**	还 要 **hái yào**	汤吗？ **tāng**	**ma?**	还 要 **Hái yào**	酸辣汤。 **suānlà-tāng.**
Do you want more soup?				Yes, (I) want more hot-and-sour soup.	
		菜 **cài**			那个菜 **nà ge cài**
		米饭 **mǐfàn**			米饭 **mǐfàn**
		面条 **miàntiáo**			鸡蛋面 **jīdànmiàn**
	吃 **chī**			吃 **chī**	面条和饼 **miàntiáo hé bǐng**
	吃肉 **chī ròu**			吃 **chī**	牛肉 **niúròu**

Pronunciation Note: Tonal modification: The half-3rd tone at the beginning

When a 3rd tone is by itself it is pronounced as a full 3rd tone. But when a 3rd tone is at the beginning of a word or compound and is followed by a different tone (1st, 2nd, or 4th tone), the 3rd tone is pronounced as a half-3rd tone, which falls but does not rise. The printed tone mark does not change. For example, in the following compounds, měi is pronounced as a short, half 3rd tone.

Pinyin	Chinese	English
měi tiān	每天	every day
měi nián	每年	every year
měi yuè	每月	every month

Pronunciation Practice

Read the following words and phrases with initial 3rd tones aloud.

Pinyin	Characters	English
1. wǒ chī	我吃	I eat
2. wǒ lái	我来	I will come
3. wǒ yào	我要	I want
4. nǐ hē	你喝	you drink
5. nǐ lái	你来	you will come
6. nǐ huàn	你换	you change
7. wǔ tiān	五天	five days
8. wǔ nián	五年	five years
9. wǔ cì	五次	five times
10. lǎoshī	老师	teacher

Practice these words that have 3rd tones followed by 2nd tones.

Pinyin	Characters	English
1. Měiguó	美国	United States
2. lǎorén	老人	old person
3. zhǎoqián	找钱	give change
4. gǎigé	改革	to reform
5. hǎiyáng	海洋	ocean
6. yěmán	野蛮	barbarous
7. jiǎngtái	讲台	platform
8. zǒngcái	总裁	company president
9. jiějué	解决	to solve
10. jǐngchá	警察	police

Each entry below has an initial sound and a final sound that combine to form complete words. Read the initial and the final sound, then read the full word. Check your pronunciation on the audio.

Group A:	Group B:	Group C:	Group D:
zh **ē**	d **uō**	z **ài**	g **uāi**
ch **áo**	t **ú**	c **án**	k **uí**
sh **ǎng**	l **iǎo**	s **uān**	h **é**
r **ì**	n **àn**		

Practice Pinyin by reading the following terms aloud.

1. **xuéxiào** 学校 school
2. **xiǎoxué** 小学 elementary school
3. **zhōngxué** 中学 secondary school
4. **dàxué** 大学 university, college
5. **Jiàoyùbù** 教育部 Ministry of Education
6. **Jiàoyùjú** 教育局 Bureau of Education
7. **Zhōngyāng Zhèngfǔ** 中央政府 Central Government
8. **shěng** 省 province
9. **Guówùyuàn** 国务院 State Council
10. **shì** 市 city
11. **xiàn** 县 county
12. **Shāngyèbù** 商业部 Ministry of Commerce
13. **shāngdiàn** 商店 store
14. **Nóngyèbù** 农业部 Ministry of Agriculture
15. **nóngcūn** 农村 countryside
16. **Wénhuàbù** 文化部 Ministry of Culture
17. **chāojí shìchiǎng** 超级市场 / **chāoshì** 超市 supermarket
18. **shūdiàn** 书店 bookstore
19. **ziǎoshì** 早市 morning market
20. **jǐngchájú** 警察局 police bureau
21. **pàichūsuǒ** 派出所 police station
22. **gōngsī** 公司 company

23. **lǜshīsuǒ** 律师所 law firm
24. **yóujú** 邮局 post office
25. **yīwùsuǒ** 医务所 clinic
26. **yīyuàn** 医院 hospital
27. **bàngōngshì** 办公室 office
28. **lǚguǎn** 旅馆 / **fàndiàn** 饭店 / **bīnguǎn** 宾馆 hotel
29. **gōngyuán** 公园 park
30. **zhàoxiàngguǎn** 照相馆 photo shop

day: 12

How to Order

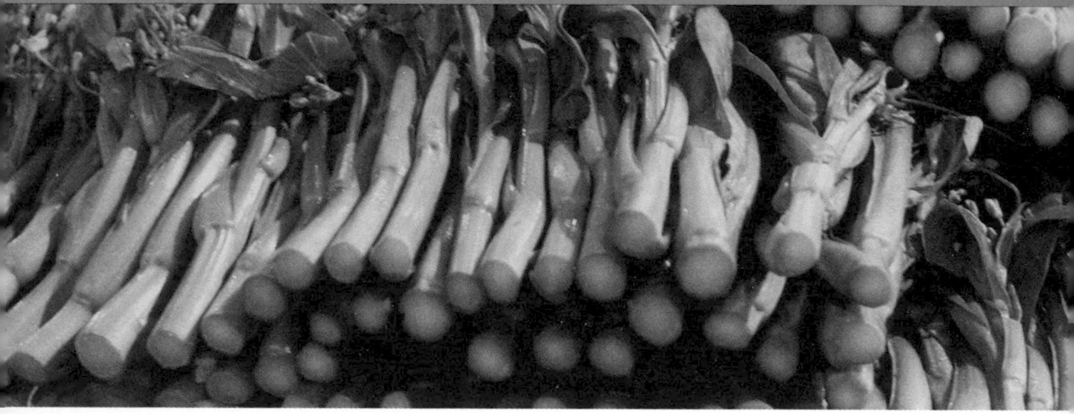

Day 12 sees you ordering food out and about. You will also learn about the etiquette if invited to someone's home for a meal and you will put into practice what you have learned in the last few lessons.

DINNER INVITES...

If you are invited to a friend or colleague's home for dinner, you should bring a gift such as fruit, wine, flowers, chocolates, cake, or toys for children. A finger towel might be offered to clean your hands before, during or after the meal, or there might only be napkins. There will likely be formal toasts before the dinner begins. The host will usually take some food from the dishes on the table and put it on your plate. It is impolite to refuse.

Exercises

Exercise 1

Read and listen to the dialogue below, and then answer the questions.

First review these new vocabulary words:

碗 **wǎn** (bowl)

找 **zhǎo** (to give change back)

At a counter 在柜台

A: Foreigner 外国人 **wàiguórén**;

B: Server 服务员 **fúwùyuán**

A: 你要什么？

B: 我要一个馒头。

A: 还要什么？

B: 还要一碗米饭。多少钱？

A: 三块钱。

B: 这是五块钱。

A: 找你两块钱。

B: 好，谢谢。

Questions:

1. What does the foreigner ask for first? ....

....

2. What else does the foreigner ask for? ....

....

3 How much is the total cost? ....

....

4. **The change the foreigner receives back is**..

....

Exercise 2

Listen to the dialogue and answer the questions. First review the word that is not in the vocabulary list for this lesson:

一共 **yígòng** (altogether, in total)

A: 我要这个菜。这个菜多少钱？

B: 这个菜两块五。

A: 那个菜多少钱？

B: 那个菜三块钱。

A: 我要一个这个菜，一个那个菜。

B: 好，一共五块五。

Questions:

1. **How many dishes does the foreigner order?**..
2. **How much is the total bill?** ....

Exercise 3

Practice ordering these dishes, saying: "我要 **Wǒ yào** ...."

菜 **cài**	鱼 **yú**	米饭 **mǐfàn**
鸡 **jī**	牛肉 **niúròu**	馒头 **mántou**

Exercise 4

Write the names of the following foods in Pinyin in the blanks.

1. **fish** ....
2. **chicken** ....
3. **noodles** ....
4. **beef** ....

Exercise 5

To prepare to buy food at a cafeteria in China, translate these sentences into Chinese. Write your answers in Pinyin.

1. **Is this a beef dish?** ....
....
2. **I don't want this dish. I want that dish.** ....
....
3. **I would like egg-drop soup .** ....
....
4. **I also want four steamed buns.** ....
....
5. **I don't want any more, thank you.** ....
....

day: 13

Deciphering the Menu

Day 13 is a vocabulary booster for food and eating out. Take the time to learn all these everyday useful words and phrases.

BANQUETS...

A foreign guest sometimes has the chance to attend a formal banquet. Some points to note are: There are usually three glasses in front of each person: a small glass for ***Máotái*** *(a well-known brand of strong liquor), a stemmed glass for wine, and a glass for water or soft drinks. The host gives the first toast, usually with wine, instead of the higher alcohol-content* ***Máotái****, to symbolize friendship. At a formal banquet only the highest-ranking host will go around to the other tables to toast. All the other people should stay at their table and toast only the people at that table. When toasting, your glass should be held a little lower than the other person's to show respect.*

A finger towel will be offered three times during the banquet for you to clean your hands – when you sit down, after eating and at the end.

Vocabulary

Key Expressions

你们有什么菜？
Nǐmen yǒu shénme cài?
What dishes do you have?

我吃素。有素菜吗？
Wǒ chīsù. Yǒu sùcài ma?
I am a vegetarian. Do you have vegetarian dishes?

小姐！买单。
Xiǎojie! Mǎidān.
Waitress! The check, please.

一共多少钱？
Yígòng duōshao qián?
How much is it altogether?

New Words I • 生词一

Characters	Pinyin	English
饭馆(儿)	**fànguǎn(r)**	*restaurant*
进	**jìn**	*to enter, to come in*
这边	**zhèbian**	*this side, over here*
边	**biān**	*side, edge*
坐	**zuò**	*to sit*
美国人	**Měiguórén**	*American (person)*
我们	**wǒmen**	*we, us*
英国人	**Yīngguórén**	*British person*
(一)点儿	**(yì)diǎnr**	*a little; some*
菜单	**càidān**	*menu*
来	**lái**	*to bring; to come, to arrive*
炒	**chǎo**	*to stir-fry*
炒鸡丁	**chǎojī-dīng**	*stir-fried diced hicken with diced vegetables*

鸡丁	**jīdīng**	*diced chicken*
丁	**dīng**	*cube, diced piece*
糖	**táng**	*sugar, sweets, candy*
醋	**cù**	*vinegar*
糖醋	**tángcù**	*sweet-and-sour (things)*
片	**piàn**	*slice, thin piece*
葱	**cōng**	*green onion*
爆	**bào**	*to quick-fry, to explode*
葱爆	**cōngbào**	*quick-fried with green onion*
没	**méi**	*not; to not have* (short form of 没有 **méiyǒu**)
没有	**méiyǒu**	*to not have*
先	**xiān**	*first; before*
这些	**zhèxie**	*these*
些	**xiē**	*some, a few, a little*

Dialogue I • 对话一

Roles

A: Customer 顾客 **gùkè;**
B: Waitress/waiter 小姐 **xiǎojie** / 师傅 **shīfu**

B: 请进。请这边坐。 **Qǐng jìn. Qǐng zhèbian zuò.**
A: 谢谢。 **Xièxie.**
B: 你们是美国人吗？ **Nǐmen shì Měiguórén ma?**
A: 不是。我们是英国人。 **Búshì. Wǒmen shì Yīngguórén.**
B: 你们吃点儿什么？ **Nǐmen chī diǎnr shénme?**
A: 你们有什么菜？ **Nǐmen yǒu shénme cài?**
B: 这是菜单。 **Zhè shì càidān.**
A: 好。来一个炒鸡丁，一个糖醋鱼片，一个酸辣汤。有没 有葱爆牛肉？ **Hǎo. Lái yí ge chǎojīdīng, yí ge tángcù yúpiàn, yí ge suānlàtāng. Yǒu méiyǒu cōngbào niúròu?**
B: 没有。 **Méiyǒu.**
A: 先要这些。谢谢。 **Xiān yào zhèxie. Xièxie.**

Translation of Dialogue I

B: Please come in. Please sit here.
A: Thank you.
B: What would you like to order?
A: What dishes do you have.
B: Here is the menu.
A: OK. Please bring one stir-fried diced chicken, one sweet-and-sour sliced fish, and one hot-and-sour soup. Do you have quick-fried beef with green onions?
B: No.
A: I'll have these first. Thank you.
B: Thank you.
A: You're welcome.

请 **qǐng** *(please, to invite)* is used in the dialogue before the main verb of an imperative sentence in order to be polite.

请进。

Qǐng jìn.
Come in, please.
请坐。
Qǐng zuò.
Sit down, please.

请 **qǐng** can also be used alone to politely invite people to come in, sit down, eat or drink, etc., according to the context.

请！请！
Qǐng. Qǐng.
Please [sit down]. Please [have more].
请多来点儿。
Qǐng duō lái diǎnr.
Please have more.

这边 **zhèbian** *(on this side)* (or **zhèbianr** in Beijing) is a place word that usually comes before the verb in a sentence. You can also put 在 **zài** as a preposition before the place word without any change of meaning:

请这边坐。
Qǐng zhèbian zuò.
Please sit on this side.
请在这边坐。
Qǐng zài zhèbian zuò.
Please sit on this side.
一个炒鸡丁，
yí ge chǎojīdīng
one stir-fried diced chicken
一个糖醋鱼片
yí ge tángcù yúpiàn
one sweet-and-sour sliced fish

The measure word 个 **ge**, as a generic measure word for many objects, can be used for ordering food dishes in a restaurant. Otherwise 盘 **pán** is the measure word for food dishes.

New Words II • 生词二

Characters	Pinyin	English
吃素	**chīsù**	*vegetarian; to eat only vegetables*
素	**sù**	*plain; vegetable*
素菜	**sùcài**	*vegetable dish*
炒鸡蛋	**chǎojīdàn**	*scrambled eggs*
喝	**hē**	*to drink*
饮料	**yǐnliào**	*drinks, beverages*
茶	**chá**	*tea*
咖啡	**kāfēi**	*coffee*
冷饮	**lěngyǐn**	*cold drink(s)*
啤酒	**píjiǔ**	*beer*
杯	**bēi**	*cup, glass*
可乐	**kělè**	*cola* (short for 可口可乐 **Kěkǒu Kělè**)
水	**shuǐ**	*water*
瓶	**píng**	*bottle*
买单	**mǎidān**	*bill/check* (in a restaurant or bar only)
一共	**yígòng**	*altogether, in total*
杯子	**bēizi**	*cup*
盘子	**pánzi**	*plate*
碗	**wǎn**	*bowl*
筷子	**kuàizi**	*chopsticks*
勺子	**sháozi**	*spoon*
叉子	**chāzi**	*fork*
宫保	**gōngbǎo**	*a spicy, diced meat dish*

Dialogue II • 对话二

Roles

A:	Customer	顾客 **gùkè;**
B:	Waitress/waiter	小姐 **xiǎojie**

A:	我吃素。有素菜吗？	**Wǒ chīsù. Yǒu sùcài ma?**
B:	有炒鸡蛋，炒素菜。	**Yǒu chǎojīdàn, chǎosùcài.**
A:	我要一个炒素菜。	**Wǒ yào yí ge chǎosùcài.**
B:	你们喝什么饮料？	**Nǐmen hē shénme yǐnliào?**
A:	你们有什么？	**Nǐmen yǒu shénme?**
B:	茶，咖啡，冷饮 和 啤酒 都 有。	**Chá, kāfēi, lěngyǐn hé píjiǔ dōu yǒu.**
A:	要两杯可乐，一杯水，一瓶啤酒。	**Yào liǎng bēi kělè, yì bēi shuǐ, yì píng píjiǔ. Zhè shì càidān.**
A:	小姐！买单。一共多少钱？	**Xiǎojie! Mǎidān. Yígòng duōshao qián?**
B:	一共一百二十五块。	**Yígòng yìbǎi èrshíwǔ kuài.**
A:	谢谢。	**Xièxie.**

Translation of Dialogue I

A: I am a vegetarian. Do you have vegetarian dishes?
B: We have scrambled eggs and stir-fried vegetable dishes.
A: I want to order a stir-fried vegetable dish.
B: What would you like to drink?
A: What kind of drinks do you have?
B: We have tea, coffee, cold drinks, and beer.
A: We'd like two glasses of cola, one glass of water, and one bottle of beer.

A: Miss! The check, please. How much is the total?
A: Altogether it is 125 yuan.
B: Thank you.

没有 **méiyǒu** *(to not have)* is the only negative form of 有 **yǒu** *(to have)*. Notice that 不 **bù** is never used with 有 **yǒu**.

day: 14

At a Restaurant

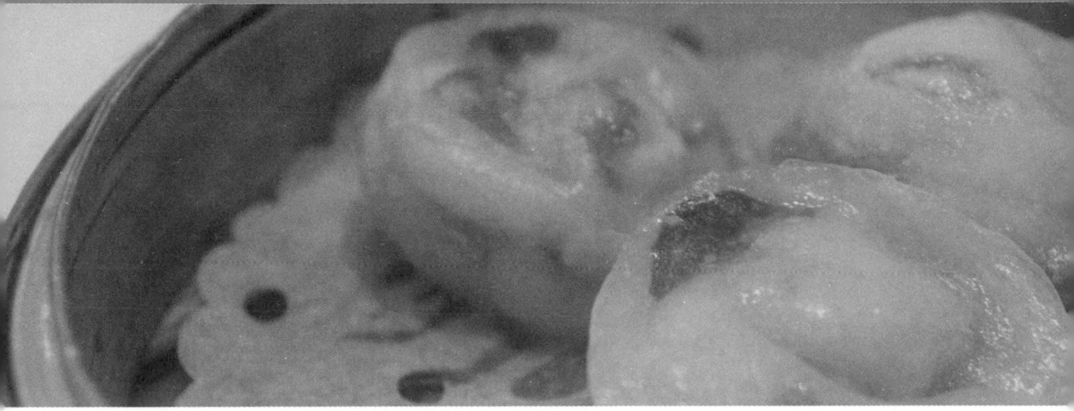

Day 14 sees you go to a restaurant. You will learn about tipping and how to ask what they have, what you want and how to express that you want a little of something. You will also learn how to form sentences with the subject omitted. Finally, you will focus on some pronunciation practice.

TIPS (小费 XIǍOFÈI)...

There is traditionally no tipping in Chinese restaurants. However, restaurants in high-end hotels often add a 15 percent service charge to the bill.

Grammar

The adverb (一) 点儿 (yì) diǎnr

点儿 **diǎnr** *(a little)* usually follows a verb to indicate "*doing something a little.*" 吃点儿什么？**Chī diǎnr shénme?** *(What would you like to eat?)* literally means *What would you like to eat a little?* 点儿 **diǎnr** is a shortened form of 一点儿 **yìdiǎnr** *(a little)* with 一 **yì** (a) omitted; it modifies 什么 **shénme** *(what)* in the example above.

Sentences with subjects omitted

In Chinese the subject of a sentence can often be omitted when the context makes clear who or what the subject is.

A:	有素菜吗？ **Yǒu sùcài ma?**	Do you have vegetarian dishes?
B:	有。 **Yǒu.**	Yes, we do.

The adverb 一共 yígòng

The adverb 一共 **yígòng** *(altogether, in total)* is used only with numbers and must be put immediately before the number.

一共一百二十五块。 **Yígòng yìbǎi èrshíwǔ kuài.**	Altogether 125 yuan.

What would you like to eat?

吃点儿什么？**Chī diǎn shénme?** *(What would you like to eat?)* is a very common first question for a server to ask a customer in a Chinese restaurant.

Question				Answer		
Subject	*Verb*	**diǎnr**	*Int.*	*Subject*	*Verb*	*Object*
你们	吃	点儿	什么？	我	要	炒鸡丁。
Nǐmen	**chī**	**diǎnr**	**shénme?**	**Wǒ**	**yào**	**chǎojīdīng.**
What would you like to eat?				I would like stir-fried diced chicken.		

Practice asking and answering questions with this pattern using the verbs and objects provided.

Subject	*Verb*	**diǎnr**	*Int.*	*Subject*	*Verb*	*Object*
	喝 **hē**				喝 **hē**	水 **shuǐ**
	要 **yào**				要 **yào**	糖醋鱼 **tángcùyú**
	来 **lái**				来个 **lái ge**	炒鸡蛋 **chǎojīdàn**

You can add information after 什么 **shénme** to make the question more specific. For example: 你们吃点儿什么菜？ **Nǐmen chī diǎnr shénme cài?** *(What dishes would you like to eat?)*

Practice asking and answering questions with this pattern:

Question				Answer		
Subject	*Verb*	**diǎnr**	*Int.*	*Subject*	*Verb*	*Object*
	喝 **hē**	什么饮料？ **shénme yǐnliào?**			要 **yào**	可乐 **kělè**
	要 **yào**	什么菜？ **shénme cài**			来个 **lái ge**	素菜 **sùcài**

Do you have ...?

有 **Yǒu ...** 吗 **ma?** *(Do you have ...?)* is a sentence pattern with the subject omitted. It is used very often in restaurants, shops, and markets.

Yǒu	*Object*	*ma*
有 **Yǒu**	咖啡 **kāfēi**	吗？ **ma?**

Do you have coffee?

The negative answer to this question is 没有。 **Méiyǒu.** *(No, I don't have ...)*

Practice making new sentences with this pattern using the objects provided:

米饭
mǐfàn

葱爆牛肉
cōngbào niúròu
炒素菜
chǎo sùcài
茶
chá
面条
miàntiáo

Do you have ...?

有没有 **Yǒu méiyǒu ...?** *(Do you have ...?)* is an affirmative-negative question. It is formed by combining the positive verb 有 **yǒu** with the negative verb 没有 **méiyǒu**. The answer can be either 有 **yǒu** *(yes, to have)* or 没有 **méiyǒu** *(no, to not have)*. This question form is frequently used in daily life in China. The meaning of 有没有 **Yǒu méiyǒu ...?** is the same as 有 **Yǒu ...** 吗 **ma?**

有没有	素菜？	有。/没有。
Yǒu méiyǒu	**sùcài?**	**Yǒu. / Méiyǒu.**
Do you have vegetarian dishes?		Yes, we do. / No, we don't.

Practice asking and answering questions with this pattern using the objects provided.

Object	*Answer*
可乐 **kělè**	no
汤面 **tāngmiàn**	yes
炒鸡蛋 **chǎojīdàn**	no
牛肉 **niúròu**	yes
啤酒 **píjiǔ**	no
炒肉丁 **chǎoròudīng**	yes

What do you have?

有什么 **Yǒu shénme ...?** *(What do you have?)* can be used to ask what kinds of food you can order.

Question				Answer		
Subject	*Verb*	*Int.*	*Object*	*Subject*	*Verb*	*Object*
你们	有	什么	菜？	我们	有	鸡，鱼，肉。
Nǐmen	**yǒu**	**shénme**	**cài ?**	**Wǒmen**	**yǒu**	**jī, yú, ròu.**

Practice asking and answering questions using this pattern with the objects provided below.

Object: Question	*Object: Answer*
鸡 **jī**	炒 鸡丁 **chǎojīdīng**
鱼 **yú**	糖醋鱼 **tángcùyú**
肉 **ròu**	葱爆牛肉 **cōngbào niúròu**
菜 **cài**	炒素菜 **chǎosùcài**
啤酒 **píjiǔ**	美国啤酒 **Měiguó píjiǔ**
饮料 **yǐnliào**	可乐 和水 **kělè hé shuǐ**

How much is it?

Use 一共 **yígòng** to ask how much the bill is, and then answer with the amount.

Question		Answer	
Total is	*Int.*	*Total is*	*Number*
一共	多少钱？	一共	三十五 块。
Yígòng	**duōshao qián?**	**Yígòng**	**sānshíwǔ kuài.**
			¥15.50
			¥7.25

¥133.40

¥54.30

¥200

¥10.12

Pronunciation Note: The letter "e"

There are two pronunciations of the letter "e": the central vowel and the high front vowel.

1. The central vowel pronunciation is like the pronunciation of "*uh*," where the lips are spread and sound is coming from the throat. Be sure to spread your lips instead of rounding them, which is the common tendency when English speakers first try to pronounce this sound. The central vowel pronunciation is used when "e" occurs in the following three instances:

a. "e" alone as an independent syllable

Pinyin	*Chinese*	*English*
***É*guó**	俄国	Russia
Wǒ *è* le.	我饿了。	I am hungry.

b. "e" as the final of a syllable

Pinyin	*Chinese*	*English*
h*é*	河	river
ch*ē*	车	vehicle, car
wǒd*e*	我的	mine, my
D*é*guó	德国	Germany
D*é*zhōu	德州	Texas

c. "e" in the final "en" or "eng"

Pinyin	*Chinese*	*English*
Ēn	恩	kindness, grace
gēn	根	root, end
zhēn	真	real
dēng	灯	light
zhēng	蒸	to steam

2. The high front vowel "e" pronunciation is like the American English pronunciation of "h*a*y." It is used when "e" is in a diphthong.

Pinyin	*Chinese*	*English*
měi [like English "may"]	美	beautiful
hēi [like English "hay"]	黑	black
bēizi	杯子	cup
Chūnjié	春节	the Spring Festival

Pronunciation Practice

Read the following words aloud. Be careful to pronounce the central vowel "e" and the front high vowel "e" correctly.

"e" alone as an independent syllable:

1. **Éguo**	俄国	Russia
2. **ézi**	蛾子	moth
3. **étou**	额头	forehead
4. **Wǒ è le.**	我饿了。	I am hungry.

"e" as the final of a syllable:

5. **shé**	蛇	snake
6. **kuàilè**	快乐	happy
7. **qìchē**	汽车	automobile
8. **zhèngcè**	政策	policy
9. **Huánghé**	黄河	the Yellow River
10. **tèkuài**	特快	express train

11. **Kěkǒu Kělè**	可口可乐	Coca-Cola®
12. **Déguó**	德国	Germany
13. **Dézhōu**	德州	Texas
14. **Búkèqi**	不客气	You are too polite. You're welcome.

"e" in the final "en" or "eng":		
15. **shén**	神	god, deity, divinity
16. **mén**	门	door
17. **Ménggǔ**	蒙古	Mongolia
18. **mèng**	梦	dream
19. **hěn hǎo**	很好	very good
20. **néng**	能	can, able to

"e" in a diphthong:		
21. **mèimei**	妹妹	younger sister
22. **gěi**	给	to give
23. **Běijīng**	北京	Beijing
24. **zéi**	贼	thief
25. **jiějie**	姐姐	older sister
26. **tiělù**	铁路	railway
27. **zhédié**	折叠	to fold
28. **dǎliè**	打猎	to hunt

Here are more words that contain the vowel "e". Read them aloud, being careful to pronounce the central vowel "e" and the front high vowel "e" correctly.

Pinyin	Chinese	English
1. **xiǎojie**	小姐	Miss
2. **hē shuǐ**	喝水	to drink water
3. **wǔ fēn**	五分	five fen
4. **Měiguó**	美国	America
5. **gēge**	哥哥	older brother
6. **Éhài'é**	俄亥俄	Ohio
7. **xiǎofèi**	小费	tip

8. huǒchē	火车	train
9. cèsuǒ	厕所	restroom
10. fēng	风	wind
11. shéngzi	绳子	rope

Each entry below has an initial sound and a final sound that combine to form complete words. Read the initial and final sounds separately, then read the full word. Check your pronunciation on the audio.

Group A:		Group B:		Group C:		Group D:	
b	**ēi**	zh	**è**	j	**iǔ**	z	**ài**
p	**ō**	ch	**ǎo**	q	**iàn**	c	**ōng**
m	**án**	sh	**í**	x	**iāng**	s	**ù**
f	**áng**	r	**éng**				

Read the following names of fruits and vegetables aloud.

1. **guā** 瓜 melon, squash
2. **guǎnggān** 广柑 grapefruit
3. **kǔguā** 苦瓜 bitter gourd
4. **kōngxīncài** 空心菜 a hollow stemmed green vegetable
5. **huángguā** 黄瓜 cucumber
6. **húluóbù** 胡萝卜 carrot
7. **yángcōng** 洋葱 onion
8. **yángbáicài** 洋白菜 cabbage
9. **wāndòu** 豌豆 peas
10. **wōsǔn** 莴笋 Chinese asparagus
11. **zhīmá** 芝麻 sesame
12. **zhúsǔn** 竹笋 bamboo shoots
13. **cándòu** 蚕豆 broad bean
14. **càihuā** 菜花 cauliflower

day: 15

Eating Out

Day 15 is all about further improving your speech and conversation skills. You are now half-way through the course and should be gaining confidence every day.

TYPES OF FOOD IN CHINA...

*The two basic categories of restaurants are Chinese-style (中餐 **zhōngcān**) and Western-style (西餐 **xīcān**). There are many Chinese restaurants named after local cuisine. For instance, "Peking duck" (北京烤鸭 **Běijīng kǎoyā**). "Sichuan-style" (四川风味 **Sìchuān fēngwèi**) restaurants serve spicy food from Sichuan. "Guangdong-style" (粤菜 **Yuècài**) or **Gǎngcài** (港菜 **Gǎngcài** Hong Kong–style) restaurants serve dimsum and other specialties. 韩国烧烤 **Hánguó shāokǎo** restaurants sell Korean barbecue and food, and 日本料理 **Rìběn liàolǐ** restaurants serve Japanese cuisine. 家常菜 **jiā cháng cài** means* family style, *and usually serve northern-style food.*

Exercises

Exercise 1

Listen to the dialogue below, then answer the questions.

First study this new vocabulary word:

羊肉 **yángròu** (lamb)

A: Customer 顾客 **gùkè**;

B: Waiter 师傅 **shīfu**

B: 请进，请这边坐。

A: 谢谢。

B: 您吃点儿什么？

A: 你们有什么菜？

B: 鸡，鱼，肉都有。

A: 你们有什么肉？

B: 有猪肉，牛肉，羊肉。

A: 我要一个羊肉。

Questions:

1. **What did the customer ask the waiter first?** ....

....

....

2. **What did the customer ask the waiter after that?** ....

....

....

3. **What did the customer finally order?** ....

....

....

Exercise 2

Listen to the dialogue, then answer the questions.

First study these new vocabulary words:

茶 **chá** (tea) 壶 **hú** (pot)

A: Customer 顾客 **gùkè**;

B: Waiter 师傅 **shīfu**

B: 您喝什么？

A: 你们有什么？

B: 我们有啤酒，有汽水。

A: 我不要啤酒。有茶吗？

B: 有茶。

A: 我要一壶茶。

Questions:

1. What did the waiter ask the customer? ....

....

....

2. What beverage did the waiter offer? ....

....

....

3. What did the customer want? ....

....

....

Exercise 3

It's your turn to order a meal in Chinese! Choose three dishes that you would like to order from the menu below. Tell the waiter/waitress what you would like, then ask how much it will cost.

Example:

A. Waiter/waitress: 你们吃点儿什么？
Nǐmen chī diǎnr shénme?

B. Customer: 来一个 …
Lái yí ge....
一共多少钱？
Yígòng duōshao qián?

菜单 MENU	
素菜 **Sùcài**	
炒素菜 **chǎosùcài**	¥6.00
炒鸡蛋 **chǎojīdàn**	¥5.00
素烧豆腐 **sùsh āo dòufu**	¥7.00
肉菜 **Ròucài**	
葱爆牛肉 **cōngbào níuròu**	¥16.00
炒鸡丁 **chǎojīdīng**	¥14.00
炒三丁 **chǎosāndīng**	¥12.00
炒肉片 **chǎoròupiàn**	¥18.00

Exercise 4

You are about to go to dinner at a Chinese restaurant with some friends. To prepare, translate the following sentences into Chinese. Write them in Pinyin or characters.

1. **What dishes do you have?** ....

....

....

2. **Two of us are vegetarians. Do you have vegetarian dishes?** ....

....

....

3. **Please bring us two glasses of beer, one cola and one water. (来 lái *bring*)** ....

....

....

4. **We would like to order three dishes: one quick-fried beef with onions, one fish and one vegetable dish.** ....

....

....

5. **Miss, the check please. How much is it altogether? (一共 yígòng *altogether*)** ....

....

....

day: 16

On the Phone

Day 16 teaches you how to make phone calls in Mandarin. You will learn the vocabulary you need to speak on the phone as well as hear some telephone dialogues with native speakers to help you build your comprehension and dialogue skills.

SAYING TELEPHONE NUMBERS

*In China you should say each digit in a phone number separately. For instance, 800 is said "eight, zero, zero" (**not** "eight hundred"), and 3159 is said as "three, one, five, nine" (**not** "thirty-one, fifty-nine"). Remember that in reading a telephone number, "1" is often pronounced **yāo** rather than **yī**.*

Vocabulary

Key Expressions

怎么给美国打电话？ **Zěnme gěi Měiguó dădiànhuà?**	*How do I make a call to the United States?*
请告诉她给我回电话。 **Qǐng gàosu tā gěi wǒ huí diànhuà.**	*Please tell her to call me back.*
您贵姓？ **Nín guì xìng?**	*What's your surname?*
我姓…/我叫… **Wǒ xìng…/Wǒ jiào…**	*My surname is. . ./My full name is. . .*
您的电话是多少号？ **Nínde diànhuà shì duō shǎo hào?**	*What's your phone number?*

New Words I • 生词一

Characters	Pinyin	English
怎么	**zěnme**	*how, in what way*
给	**gěi**	*to; for (when transferring something to someone); to give*
美国	**Měiguó**	*United States*
打	**dă**	*to make (a phone call); to hit, to beat; to play (ball)*
电话	**diànhuà**	*telephone*
打电话	**dă diànhuà**	*to make a phone call*
拨	**bō**	*to dial (a rotary phone)*
再	**zài**	*again, still*
地区	**dìqū**	*area, region*
号	**hào**	*number, code, size*

分	**fēn**	*minute*
分钟	**fēnzhōng**	*minute*
钟	**zhōng**	*clock, o'clock*
太	**tài**	*too, excessively, extremely*
贵	**guì**	*expensive, valuable, honored*
用	**yòng**	*to use*
电话卡	**diànhuàkǎ**	*telephone card*
卡	**kǎ**	*card*
买	**mǎi**	*to buy*
邮局	**yóujú**	*post office*
商店	**shāngdiàn**	*shop, store*
商	**shāng**	*business; a surname/ last name*
店	**diàn**	*shop, store*
卖	**mài**	*to sell*

Dialogue I • 对话一

Roles

A: Foreigner 外国人 **wàiguórén;**
B: Attendant 服务员 **fúwùyuán**

A:	请问，怎么给美国打电话？	**Qǐng wèn, zěnme gěi Měiguó dǎ diànhuà?**
B:	先拨001，再拨地区号和电话号。	**Xiān bō líng líng yāo[1], zài bō dìqūhào hé diànhuàhào.**
A:	多少钱 一分钟？	**Duōshǎo qián yì fēnzhōng?**
B:	八块。	**Bā kuài.**
A:	太贵了。	**Tài guì le.**
B:	用电话卡不太贵。两块 四一分钟。	**Yòng diànhuàkǎ bú tài guì. Liǎng kuài sì yì fēnzhōng.**
A:	在哪儿买？	**Zài nǎr mǎi?**
B:	邮局和商店都卖。	**Yóujú hé shāngdiàn dōu mài.**

1. The number "1" in a telephone number (or a street address, etc.) is often pronounced **yāo** rather than **yī**.

Translation of Dialogue I

A: Excuse me, how can I make a phone call to the United States?
B: First dial 001, and then dial the area code and the number.
A: How much is it per minute?
B: Eight yuan.
A: That's too expensive.
B: It is not too expensive to use a phone card. (It's) two yuan and forty fen per minute.
A: Where can I buy one?
B: At the post office or in stores.

打电话 **dǎ diànhuà** is the only way in Chinese to say to make a phone call; it is a "verb + object" construction. 打 **dǎ** is a verb with the primary meaning of *to hit* or *to beat*, but it is also widely used in "verb + object" constructions for actions such as *to make a call*, *to buy a ticket*, or *to play ball*.

拨 **bō** *(to dial)* means to dial a rotary telephone:

先拨 001。 **Xiān bō líng líng yāo.**	First dial 001.

If the telephone has push buttons, it's better to say 按 **àn** *(to press)*:

请先按 001。 **Qǐng xiān àn líng líng yāo.**	Please first dial 001.

分钟 **fēnzhōng** *(minute)*

分 **fēn** is a unit of time and means *minute*. 钟 **zhōng** is a noun that means *clock* or, as here, *time according to the clock*. 一分钟 **yì fēnzhōng** is *one minute*. 分 **fēn** as a unit word is also used for *money*; for example, 一分钱 **yì fēn qián** is *one fen*.

卡 **kǎ** is a phonetic translation of *card*. It is added to some other words to form new nouns, such as 信用卡 **xìnyòngkǎ** *(credit card)*, 提款卡 **tíquǎnkǎ** *(debit card)* or 卡片 **kǎpiàn** *(name card)*. 卡 **kǎ** is also a phonetic translation of car, as in 卡车 **kǎchē** *(truck)*.

New Words II • 生词二

Characters	Pinyin	English
新	**xīn**	*new, fresh*
园	**yuán**	*garden*
宾馆	**bīnguǎn**	*hotel, guesthouse*
喂	**wèi**	*hello (used on the telephone or to get someone's attention)*
找	**zhǎo**	*to look for, to seek; to give change (also, "I want to speak to ...")*
谁	**shéi/shuí**	*Who?*
房间	**fángjiān**	*room*
的	**de**	*(function word)*
她	**tā**	*she, her*
告诉	**gàosu**	*to tell, to inform, to let know*

回	**huí**	*to return, to go back*
贵姓	**guì xìng**	*Your surname, please?*
姓	**xìng**	*to be surnamed; surname, family name*
叫	**jiào**	*to be called, to call out*
您的	**nínde**	*yours (polite form)*
你的	**nǐde**	*yours (informal)*
我的	**wǒde**	*my, mine*
不客气	**búkèqi**	*You're welcome.*
新园宾馆	**Xīnyuán Bīnguǎn**	*Xinyuan Hotel*
马丽莎	**Mǎ Lìshā**	*(name of a person)*
护照	**hùzhào**	*passport*

Dialogue II • 对话二

Roles

A: Foreigner — 外国人 **wàiguórén;**
B: Hotel attendant — 服务员 **fúwùyuán**

A:	喂,是新园宾馆吗？	**Wèi, shì Xīnyuán Bīnguǎn ma?**
B:	是，您找谁？	**Shì, nín zhǎo shéi?**
A:	我找314房间的马丽莎。	**Wǒ zhǎo sān yāo sì fángjiān de Mǎ Lìshā[1].**
B:	她不在。	**Tā bú zài.**
A:	请告诉她给我回电话。	**Qǐng gàosu tā gěi wǒ huí diànhuà.**
B:	请问您贵姓？	**Qǐng wèn, nín guì xìng?**
A:	我姓商,叫商美英。	**Wǒ xìng Shāng, jiào Shāng Měiyīng.**
B:	您的电话是多少号？	**Nínde diànhuà shì duōshǎo hào?**
A:	我的电话是 6725–4831。谢谢！	**Wǒde diànhuà shì liù qī èr wǔ–sì bā sān yāo. Xièxie!**
B:	不客气。	**Búkèqi.**

1. 丽莎 **Lìshā** is the Chinese pronunciation of *"Lisa."*

Translation of Dialogue II

A: Hello. Is this the Xinyuan Hotel?
B: Whom are you calling?
A: I am looking for Ma Lisha in room 314.
B: She is not in.
A: Please tell her to call me back.
B: What's your surname?
A: My surname is Shang and my full name is Shang Meiying.
B: What is your number?
A: My number is 6725-4831. Thank you.
B: You're welcome.

day: 17

Dialogues

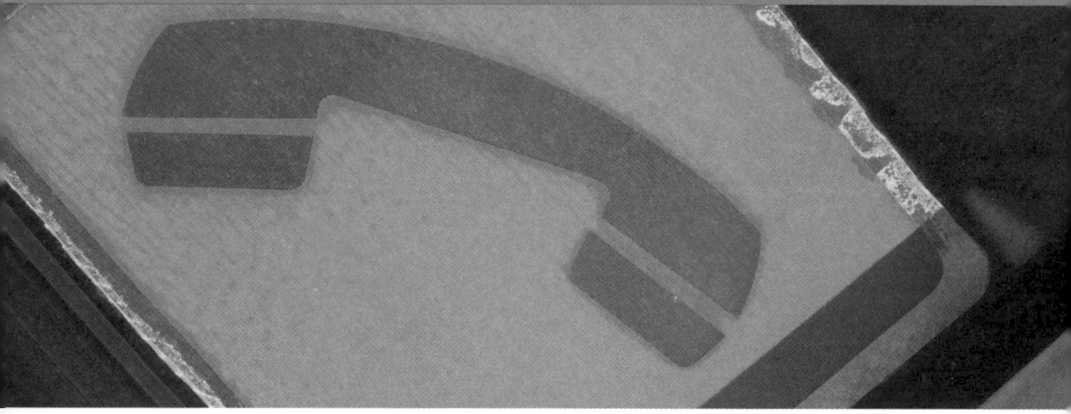

Day 17 focuses on grammar and teaches you how to form questions and use prepostions as well as some pronunciation practice.

PUBLIC PHONES

*There are public phones on the street, at train stations, and in stores. Look for the sign 公用电话 **gōngyòng diànhuà** (public phone). There are coin or card-operated public phones, but most public phones have an attendant whom you pay after you make a call. IP phone cards or 200 phone cards can be used to make calls at home and in hotel rooms. They can be used for both local and long-distance calls. They are much cheaper for international calls than any other method. You can buy them in stores, at post offices, and in hotel business centers. Before you use the card you must scratch off the covering from the code number. On the next page, you can see a typical 200 (IP) phone card. Here is a translation of the instructions on the back of a typical card.*

Grammar

她 tā (she)

In modern Chinese, the pronoun 她 **tā** means *she* and the pronoun 他 **tā** means *he*. Traditionally, however, all pronouns in Chinese were gender neutral.

她 **tā** is a new character that was created only in the twentieth century when Chinese intellectuals wanted to translate she from Western languages. Many people still write 他 whether referring to a man or a woman.

The interrogative 怎么 zěnme (how)

怎么 **zěnme** *(how)* is an interrogative adverb that is used to ask the manner or method of an action. 怎么 **zěnme** must be located before the main verb of the sentence:

怎么换钱？ How do I exchange money?
Zěnme huàn qián?
这个怎么卖？ How do you sell this? How is this sold?
Zhè ge zěnme mài?

If there is a prepositional phrase before the main verb, 怎么 **zěnme** should be placed before the preposition:

怎么给美国打电话？ How can I make a phone call to the United States?
Zěnme gěi Měiguó dǎ diànhuà?

The preposition 给 gěi (to, toward)

In the phrase 给美国打电话 **gěi Měiguó dǎ diànhuà** *(make a phone call to the United States)*, 给 **gěi** *(to, toward)* is a preposition in the phrase 给美国 **gěi Měiguó** and is located before the main verb 打 **dǎ**. In this context, 给 **gěi** can introduce either a place or a person:

给中国打电话 to make a call to China
gěi Zhōngguó dǎ diànhuà
给北京打电话 to make a call to Beijing
gěi Běijīng dǎ diànhuà
给你打电话 to call you
gěi nǐ dǎ diànhuà

先 xiān … 再 zài … (first … then)

先 **xiān**… 再 **zài**… is used to describe two actions or events in succession. 先 **xiān** is for the first action or event; 再 **zài** is for the second:

先买电话卡，再打电话。 **Xiān mǎi diànhuàkǎ, zài dǎ diànhuà.**	Buy a phone card first, (and) then make phone calls.

太 tài … 了 le (too, excessively, extremely …)

太 **tài** is an adverb that modifies an adjective or a verb, and is used to express degree or extent. It must be placed immediately before that adjective or verb. 太 **tài** … 了 **le** is a frame that can take any adjective. For example:

太好了！**Tài hǎo le!**	It's great!
太多了！**Tài duō le!**	It's too much!
太客气了！**Tài kèqi le!**	(You're) too polite!

If an adjective is commendatory (positive), as in the above examples, the 了 **le** is required. However, if the adjective is derogatory you can simply put 太 **tài** before it, and the 了 **le** is optional. For example, both 太贵了 **tài guì le** *(too expensive)* and 太贵 **tài guì** *(too expensive)* are acceptable.

The particle 的 de

的 **de** is a function word that has many different uses in Chinese. You will learn two functions of 的 **de** in this lesson.

a. 的 **de** as a modifier marker:

的 **de** occurs very frequently after a word, a phrase, or a clause to form a 的 **de** phrase that modifies a noun. 的 **de** is used like the English *who*, *which*, or *that*.

我找314房间的马丽莎。 **Wǒ zhǎo sān yāo sì fángjiān de Mǎ Lìshā.**	I am looking for Ma Lisha who is in room 314.

b. 的 **de** shows possession:

Adding 的 **de** after a pronoun or noun makes a possessive form.

您的 **nínde**	yours (polite form)
我的 **wǒde**	my; mine
你的 **nǐ de**	yours

那是我的，不是你的。 That is mine, not yours.
Nà shì wǒde, búshì nǐde.

在 zài (to be in/at) as a verb

马小姐在吗？**Mǎ Xiǎojie zài ma?** is a standard expression that means *Is Miss Ma in?* in which 在 **zài** is used as a verb and no place word follows it. The place word is omitted because the context makes clear that the place is 这儿 **zhèr** *(here)* or 那儿 **nàr** *(there)*. The negative answer is 她不在 **Tā bú zài.** *(She is not in [here/there])*.

You have already learned 在 **zài** as a preposition. You can identify 在 **zài** as a preposition, rather than a verb, when there is a main verb in the sentence and when 在 **zài** is followed by a place word: 在 **zài** + place word + verb. Here is an example of 在 **zài** as a preposition:

我在银行换钱。 I exchange money in the bank.
Wǒ zài yínháng huàn qián.

您贵姓？Nín guì xìng? (What's your surname?)

您贵姓？**Nín guì xìng?** *(What's your surname?)* is the polite way of asking a surname, and it is a fixed expression, especially when using 您 **nín** *(you)*, the polite form of 你 **nǐ**. 贵 **guì** usually means *expensive*, but here means *honorable*, modifying 姓 **xìng** *(surname)*. 您贵姓 **Nín guì xìng?** *(What's your surname?)* is understood as a question and does not have an interrogative word.

The reply will be: 我姓 . . . **Wǒ xìng . . .** (My surname is . . .)

姓 xìng (to be surnamed; a surname)

Usually 姓 **xìng** acts as a verb. Thus in a question 姓 **xìng** is followed by 什么 **shénme** *(what)*, and in the answer it is followed by a Chinese surname:

您姓什么？ What is your surname?
Nín xìng shénme?
我姓商。 My surname is Shang.
Wǒ xìng Shāng.

The negative form is 不姓 **bú xìng**:

我不姓商;我姓张。 **Wǒ bú xìng Shāng; wǒ xìng Zhāng.**	I am not surnamed Shang; I am surnamed Zhang.

Sometimes 姓 **xìng** can act as a noun that means "surname":

欧阳是我的姓 **Ōuyáng shì wǒde xìng.**	Ouyang is my surname.

How

怎么 **zěnme** *(how)* must be before the main verb. If there is a prepositional phrase before the main verb,

怎么 **zěnme** must be placed before the preposition. For example: 怎么给美国打电话？ **Zěnme gěi Měiguó dǎ diànhuà?** *(How can I make a phone call to the United States?)*

Practice making interrogative sentences with 怎么 **zěnme**:

Zěnme	Verb	Object
怎么 **Zěnme** How do I make phone calls?	打 **dǎ**	电话？ **diànhuà?**
	换 **huàn**	钱 **qián**
	买 **mǎi**	电话卡 **diànhuàkǎ**
	炒 **chǎo**	鸡丁 **jīdīng**
	买 **mǎi**	饭票 **fànpiào** (meal ticket)
	用 **yòng**	这个 **zhè ge**
	要 **yào**	买单 **mǎidān**

First … then

先 **xiān** … 再 **zài** *(first … then)* is used to arrange two actions or events in succession. 先 **xiān** introduces the first action or event, and 再 **zài** introduces the second. Practice making new sentences with this structure.

Xiān	Verb	Object	zài	Verb	Object
先 Xiān	拨 bō	地区号， dìqūhào,	再 zài	拨 bō	电话号。 diànhuàhào.

First dial the area code, (and) then dial the telephone number.

买 **mǎi**	电话卡， **diànhuàkǎ,**	打 **dǎ**	电话 **diànhuà**
拨 **bō**	001， **línglíngyāo,**	拨 **bō**	10 **yī líng**
换 **huàn**	人民币， **Rénmínbì,**	买 **mǎi**	饭票 **fànpiào**
找 **zhǎo**	你， **ní,**	找 **zhǎo**	马丽莎 **Mǎ Lìshā**
喝 **hē**	啤酒， **píjiǔ,**	吃 **chī**	饭 **fàn**

To, for

The preposition 给 **gěi** *(to, for)* is located before the main verb in a sentence and is usually followed by a place or a person.

Practice these sentences with 给 **gěi**:

Subject	gěi + Place or person	Verb	Object
我 **Wǒ**	给她 **gěi tā**	买 **mǎi**	电话卡。 **diànhuàkǎ.**

I am buying a phone card for her.

您 **nín**	给商店 **gěi shāngdiàn**	打 **dǎ**	电话 **diànhuà**
她 **tā**	给美国 **gěi Měiguó**	回 **huí**	电话 **diànhuà**
我 **wǒ**	给你 **gěi nǐ**	买 **mǎi**	咖啡 **kāfēi**

她	给你	炒	鸡蛋
tā	**gěi nǐ**	**chǎo**	**jīdàn**

Too much

太 **tài** … 了 **le** *(too, excessively, extremely …)* is a frame with an adjective put in between 太 **tài** and 了 **le** to express a certain feeling.

Tài	Adj	le
太 **Tài**	贵 **guì**	了。 **le.**

It is too expensive.

Practice making new sentences with this pattern using the adjectives provided.

好
hǎo
多
duō
少
shǎo
客气
kèqi

Possessive with 的 de

Practice using the possessive formed by a personal pronoun or noun followed by 的 **de**:

Subject	Verb	Object
这 **Zhè**	是 **shì**	您的房间。 **nínde fángjiān.**

This is your room.

我的电话号
wǒde diànhuàhào
您的电话卡
nínde diànhuàkǎ
宾馆的电话
bīnguǎn de diànhuà

你的八百三十块人民币
nǐde bā bǎi sānshí kuài Rénmínbì
我的护照
wǒde hùzhào (passport)

在 zài (be in/at)

她不在 **Tā bú zài.** *(She is not here/there.)* is a standard expression in which 在 **zài** is used as a verb and no place word follows it.

Question			Answer
Subject	zài	ma	*Negative/Affirmative answer*
马小姐	在	吗？	不在。/ 在。
Mǎ Xiǎojie	**zài**	**ma?**	**Búzài./Zài.**
Is Miss Ma in?			(No, she is) not in./(Yes, she is) in.

Practice this pattern using the subjects below:

王老师
Wáng Lǎoshī
(teacher)
黄经理
Huáng Jīnglǐ
(manager)
主任
zhǔrèn
(office director)
校长
xiàozhǎng
(school principal)
翻译
fānyì
(translator)

To look for

找 **zhǎo** *(to look for)* is frequently used to say *I want to talk to . . . (over the phone)*, *I want to see . . . (when on a visit)*. Practice this very useful pattern.

Question			Answer		
Subject	*Verb*	*Int.*	*Subject*	*Verb*	*Object*
您	找	谁？	我	找	马小姐。
Nín	**zhǎo**	**shéi?**	**Wǒ**	**zhǎo**	**Mǎ xiǎojie.**
Who are you looking for?			I am looking for Miss Ma.		
			我		黄小姐
			wǒ		**Huáng xiǎojie**
			他		美国人
			tā		**Měiguórén**
			外国人		翻译
			wàiguórén		**fānyì** (translator)
			她经		理
			tā		**jīnglǐ** (manager)
			我		王老师
			wǒ		**Wáng lǎoshī** (Teacher Wang)

What's your surname?

When you meet a Chinese person the first time, use the polite way to ask his/her surname: 您贵姓？ **Nín guì xìng?** *What's your surname?*

The reply will be: 我姓 **Wǒ xìng . . .** *My surname is . . .*

Question			Answer		
Qǐng wèn	*Subject*	*Int.*	*Subject*	**xìng**	*Surname*
请问，	您	贵姓？	我	姓	商。
Qǐng wèn	**nín**	**guì xìng?**	**Wǒ**	**xìng**	**Shāng.**
May I ask your surname?			My surname is Shāng.		

Practice asking and answering with this pattern using the following surnames:

Question			Answer		
Qǐng wèn	*Subject*	*Int.*	*Subject*	xìng	*Surname*
					钱 **Qián**
					张 **Zhāng**
					马 **Mǎ**
					江 **Jiāng**
					王 **Wáng**

When asking for a full name say: 您叫什么？ **Nín jiào shénme?** *What's your full name?* The answer will be: 我叫 **Wǒ jiào …**

Question				Answer		
Qǐng wèn	*Subject*	jiào	*Int.*	*Subject*	xìng	*Surname*
请问，	您	叫	什么？	我	叫	商美英。
Qǐng wèn	**nín**	**jiào**	**shénme?**	**Wǒ**	**jiào**	**Shāng Měiyīng.**
May I ask your name?				I am called Shāng Měiyīng.		

Practice asking and answering with this pattern using the question subjects, answer subjects, and names provided:

Question Subj.	Answer Subj.	Full name
你 **nǐ**	我 **wǒ**	王民 **Wáng Mín**
他 **tā**	他 **tā**	张丁 **Zhāng Dīng**
她 **tā**	她 **tā**	李美 **Lǐ Měi**
那个人 **nà ge rén**	那个人 **nà ge rén**	吴用 **Wú Yòng**

Pronunciation Note: How to pronounce the initial "r"

When you say "r" in English, your lips are rounded. For example: "read," "right." But when you say "r" in Chinese, your lips should be close together and flat or spread. Your tongue is rolled upwards with the tip near the base of the upper teeth. You will feel the air vibrating around your tongue. Your lower jaw should be thrust slightly forward.

Pinyin	Chinese	English
rè	热	hot
rén	人	people
Rìběn	日本	Japan

Pronunciation Practice

Read the following words aloud. Pay careful attention to the initial "r."

Pinyin	Chinese	English
1. **ràng**	让	to allow, to let, to yield
2. **rè**	热	hot
3. **rèshuǐ**	热水	hot water
4. **rén**	人	people
5. **réngjiù**	仍旧	still
6. **suīrán**	虽然	although
7. **rènao**	热闹	bustling
8. **rénkǒu**	人口	population
9. **dǎrǎo**	打扰	to disturb
10. **wūrǎn**	污染	pollution

Read the following words aloud. These words can help you to practice your pronunciation while learning some job titles that are used every day in China.

a. Service

1. **xiǎojie** 小姐 waitress, female attendant
2. **fúwùyuán** 服务员 server

3. **shīfu** 师傅 ("master") waiter, driver, chef
4. **chúshī** 厨师 chef, cook
5. **yíngyèyuán** 营业员 service employee
6. **shòuhuòyuán** 售货员 store salesperson
7. **lǐfàshī** 理发师 barber
8. **ménwèi** 门卫 / **kānménde** 看门的 doorman
9. **sījī** 司机 driver
10. **shòupiàoyuán** 售票员 conductor, ticket clerk

b. Education

1. **yuànzhǎng** 院长 (dean)
2. **xiàozhǎng** 校长 (president, headmaster/headmistress)
3. **jiàoshòu** 教授 (professor)
4. **lǎoshī** 老师 (teacher)
5. **jiàoshī** 教师 (teacher)
6. **xuésheng** 学生 (student)
7. **dàxuésheng** 大学生 (college student)
8. **jiāzhǎng** 家长 (parents)
9. **zhōngxuésheng** 中学生 (secondary school student)
10. **kēxuéjiā** 科学家 (scientist)
11. **xiǎoxuésheng** 小学生 (elementary school student)

Sign for an IP public phone.

Can you recognize any of the characters?

day: 18

Practice

Day 18 is about practicing what you have learned so far and about speaking on the phone. Listen to the audio and write the answers as required. You can then check them at the back of the book in the Key to Exercises.

TELEPHONE CARDS

There are two basic kinds of phone cards in China: IC and IP cards. IC phone cards are only accepted in ***cíkǎ diànhuà*** *(magnetic phones). The cost is the same as other public phones, with a service fee for long distance calls. You can buy an IC card at post offices, department stores and large hotels. You cannot use an IC card to make calls at home or in a hotel room.*

Exercises

Exercise 1

Listen to the CD and fill in the blanks with what you hear in Pinyin.

1. ....

2. ....

3. ....

4. ....

5. ....

6. ....

7. ....

8. ....

9. ....

10. ....

11. ....

12. ....

13. ....

14. ....

15. ....

Exercise 2

Read and listen to the dialogue, then answer the questions below.

A: Foreigner 外国人 **wàiguórén**;

B: Hotel attendant 服务员 **fúwùyuán**

A: 请问，给美国打电话多少钱一分钟？

B: 给美国打电话三块五一分钟。

A: 给日本打电话多少钱一分钟？

B: 给日本打电话两块钱一分钟。

A: 用电话卡是不是便宜一点儿？

B: 是，用电话卡便宜。

A: 好. 谢谢。

B: 不谢。

Questions:

1. What is the rate for a call to the United States? ....

....

2. What is the rate for a call to Japan? ....

....

3. What is the cheaper way to call? ....

....

Exercise 3

Listen to the words on the CD and write them below in Pinyin.

1. ....

2. ....

3. ....

4. ....

5. ....

6. ....

7. ....

8. ....

9. ....

10. ....

Exercise 4

Fill in each blank with the appropriate measure word:

张	个	杯	瓶	块
zhāng	**gè**	**bēi**	**píng**	**kuài**

1. 我买一 ....IP卡。

   Wǒ mǎi yì .... kǎ.

2. 我换一百 .... 钱。

   Wǒ huàn yìbǎi .... qián.

3. 你要什么菜？ 我要一 ....鸡，三 .... 馒头。

   Nǐ yào shénme cài? Wǒ yào yí .... jī, sān .... mántou.

Exercise 5

Fill in each blank with the appropriate question word:

多少	哪儿	什么	谁	吗
duōshao	**nǎr**	**shénme**	**shéi**	**ma**

1. 一共 .... 钱？

   Yígòng .... qián?

2. 在 .... 买电话卡？

   Zài .... mǎi diànhuàkǎ?

3. 你们有 .... 菜？

   Nímen yǒu .... cài?

4. 请问，马丽莎在 .... ?

Qǐng wèn, Mǎ Lìshā zài .... ?

Exercise 6

You are staying in a hotel in China and want to call the United States. To prepare, translate these sentences into Chinese. Write your translations in Pinyin or characters.

1. **How do I make a phone call to the United States?** ....

....

....

2. **What number should I dial first?**..

....

....

3. **How much is it per minute to call the United States?**...

....

....

4. **That's too expensive. Where can I buy a phone card?** ....

....

....

day: 19

At the Hotel

Day 19 talks about hotels and you will build up some more vocabulary. You will refresh on how to read numbers. Listen to the dialogues to reinforce what you have learned.

CHINESE NAMES

The order of Chinese names is different from that of English names: the last name (family name or surname) comes first and the first name comes second. Chinese surnames usually have one character, for example: ***Zhào*** *赵,* ***Qián*** *钱,* ***Sūn*** *孙,* ***Lǐ*** *李,* ***Zhōu*** *周,* ***Wú*** *吴,* ***Zhèng*** *郑, and* ***Wáng*** *王. There are, however, a few two-character surnames such as* ***Ōuyáng*** *欧阳,* ***Sīmǎ*** *司马 and* ***Shàngguān*** *上官. Chinese first names usually have one or two characters. In modern China, women do not take their husband's family name when they marry.*

Vocabulary

Key Expressions

你住哪个房间？ **Nǐ zhù nǎ ge fángjiān?**	*Which room are you in?*
我需要 … **Wǒ xūyào …**	*I need …*
请等一会儿。 **Qǐng děng yí huìr.**	*Please wait a moment.*
能换床单吗？ **Néng huàn chuángdān ma?**	*Could you change my sheets?*
… 坏了。 **… huài le.**	*The … is broken.*

New Words I • 生词一

Characters	Pinyin	English
需要	**xūyào**	*to need*
条	**tiáo**	measure word for long, narrow things
毛巾	**máojīn**	*towel*
块	**kuài**	measure word for things in chunks or solid pieces
肥皂	**féizào**	*soap*
衣架	**yījià**	*hanger*
住	**zhù**	*to live, to stay*
哪个	**nǎge**	*Which? Which one?*
送	**sòng**	*to send, to deliver*
去	**qù**	*to go; away* (after a verb, indicating action directed away from the speaker)

卫生纸	**wèishēngzhǐ**	*toilet paper*
等	**děng**	*to wait*
一会儿	**yí huìr**	*in a moment, shortly, for a little while*

Dialogue I • 对话一

Roles

A: Hotel guest — 房客 **fángkè;**
B: Hotel attendant — 服务员 **fúwùyuán**

A:	小姐，我需要两条毛巾，一块 肥皂，三个衣架。	**Xiǎojie, wǒ xūyào liǎng tiáo máojīn, yí kuài féizào, sān ge yījià.**
B:	你住哪个房间？	**Nǐ zhù nǎ ge fángjiān?**
A:	405 房间。	**Sì líng wǒ fángjiān.**
B:	我 给你送去。	**Wǒ gěi nǐ sòng qù.**
A:	我要这个菜。这个菜是牛	**Wǒ hái yào wèishēngzhǐ.**
B:	我等一会儿 送去。	**Wǒ děng yí huìr sòng qù.**
A:	谢谢！	**Xièxie!**
B:	不客气。	**Búkèqi.**

Translation of Dialogue I

A: Miss, I need two towels, one bar of soap, and three hangers.
B: Which room are you in?
A: Room 405.
B: I will send them to your room.
A: I also need toilet paper.
B: I will send it to you in a moment.
A: Thank you!
B: You are welcome.

How to Read Numbers

A two-digit number is said in full, with the units (and not digit-by-digit).
For example:

18	**shíbā**
22	**èrshí èr**
96	**jǐushí liù**

A three-digit number may be said in full, with the units, or it may be said digit-by-digit:

405	**sì bǎi lǐng wǔ** or **sì lǐng wǔ**
713	**qī bǎi yīshísān** or **qī yī sān**

Four-digit numbers and above are usually said digit-by-digit, except that large round numbers may be also said in full, with the units:

17,924	**yí wàn qī qiān jiǔ bǎi èrshísì**
2002	**èr líng líng èr**
2,000	**èr líng líng líng or liǎng qiān**

给 **gěi** is a preposition meaning *to* or *for*. It is used when handing or transferring something to a person or when doing something on behalf of or for the benefit of a person. For example:

我 给 你 送 去。 I will send it over for you.
Wǒ gěi nǐ sòng qù.

This is different from the use of 给 **gěi** as a verb, meaning *to give*.

When 送 **sòng** means *to send*, *to deliver*, the person who does the action of sending must physically carry the object to a certain place. The distance of delivery can be either long or short.

Notice, however, that when someone sends a letter through the mail, the verb *send* is 寄 **jì**, not 送 **sòng**.

New Words II • 生词二

Characters	Pinyin	English
能	**néng**	*can; be able to*
打扫	**dăsăo**	*to clean, to sweep*
你的	**nĭde**	*yours*
再来	**zài lái**	*come again, come back*
现在	**xiànzài**	*now, present* (time word: always placed before the verb in a sentence.)
可以	**kěyĭ**	*may, can; may be permitted to*
床单	**chuángdān**	*bed sheets*
床	**chuáng**	*bed*
厕所	**cèsuŏ**	*bathroom, toilet*
坏	**huài**	*bad, broken, to become spoiled*
坏了	**huài le**	*to be out of order, to become spoiled*
灯	**dēng**	*light, lamp*
修	**xiū**	*to repair, to fix*

Dialogue II • 对话=

Roles

A: Hotel guest 房客 **fángkè**;
B: Hotel attendant 服务员 **fúwùyuán**

A:	谁？请等一会儿。，	**Shéi? Qǐng děng yí huìr.**
B:	能打扫你的房间 吗？	**Néng dǎsǎo nǐde fángjiān ma?**
A:	请等 一会儿再来。	**Qǐng děng yí huìr zài lái.**
A:	小姐，现在可以打扫我的房间了。请换床单。	**Xiǎojie, xiànzài kěyǐ dǎsǎo wǒde fángjiān le. Qǐng huàn chuángdān.**
B:	好。	**Hǎo.**
A:	我的厕所 坏了，灯也坏 了。	**Wǒde cèsuǒ huài le, dēng yě huài le.**
B:	一会儿给你修。	**Yí huìr gěi nǐ xiū.**

Translation of Dialogue II

A: Who is it? Just a minute, please.
B: May I clean your room?
A: Please come back later.

A: Miss, now you may clean my room. Please change the sheets.
B: OK.
A: The toilet doesn't work and the lamp is also broken.
B: We'll fix them for you shortly.

day:20

Where to Stay

Day 20 helps you to further develop your Mandarin and the gramatical components needed to express yourself more fully. You will learn how to talk about objects and use measure words.

CATEGORIES OF HOTELS

The name of a hotel in Chinese usually reveals its rating. 宾馆 ***bīnguǎn****,* 饭店 ***fàndiàn****, and* 酒店 ***jiǔdiàn*** *are usually four- or five-star hotels where most foreigners will stay. The staff in these hotels usually speaks English.* 旅馆 ***lǚguǎn*** *or* 旅店 ***lǚdiàn*** *are usually three-star (or below) hotels, and their staff usually do not speak English.* 招待所 ***zhāodàisuǒ*** *(guest houses or hostels) and* 疗养院 ***liáoyǎngyuàn*** *(health resorts) originally belonged to state-run companies or government agencies. Since the mid-1980s, with Economic Reform, most have become hotels. They usually are low-cost hotels, and only some of them let foreigners stay as guests.*

Grammar

Measure words 条 tiáo (long narrow piece) and 块 kuài (chunk)

条 **tiáo** is a measure word for things that are long and narrow in shape, such as:

两条毛巾 two towels
liǎng tiáo máojīn
一条鱼 one fish
yì tiáo yú
一条街 or 一 条路 one street
yì tiáo jiē or **yì tiáo lù**
一条裤子 one pair of pants
yì tiáo kùzi

块 **kuài** is a measure word for slices or chunks, such as:

一 块饼 a piece of fried bread
yí kuài bǐng
一块肉 a piece of meat
yí kuài ròu
一块糖 a piece of candy
yí kuài táng
一块肥皂 a bar of soap
yí kuài féizào

You have already learned that 块 **kuài** is used colloquially as a measure word for money (一块钱 **yí kuài qián**, one yuán). Originally, Chinese money was made of pieces of metal.

Simple directional complements 去 qù (away) / 来 lái (towards)

The simple directional complements 去 **qù** *(away)* and 来 **lái** *(towards)* often follow a verb to show the direction of the action relative to the speaker. Usually "main verb + 去 **qù**" indicates the action of the main verb is in the direction away from the speaker, and "main verb + 来 **lái**" indicates the action of the main verb is in the direction coming toward the speaker.

For example: 送去 **sòng qù** *(sent to)* is a phrase made up of two verbs in series. 送 **sòng** is the main verb and 去 **qù** is a secondary verb, a simple directional complement.

The adverb 一会儿 yí huìr (in a while)

等一会儿 **děng yí huìr** can mean either *to wait for a while* or else can be an expression meaning simply *in a while*. For example, 请等一会儿再来 **Qǐng děng yí huìr zài lái** means *Please come back in a while*.

Auxiliaries 能 néng (can, be able to) and 可以 kěyǐ (can, may)

In the dialogues in lesson 19, both 能 **néng** and 可以 **kěyǐ** are used to mean permitted to. They are both used before a verb:

能打扫你的房间吗？ May I clean your room?
Néng dǎsǎo nǐde fángjiān ma?
你可以打扫我的房间了。 You may clean my room now.
Nǐ kěyǐ dǎsǎo wǒde fángjiān le.

In other instances 能 **néng** *(can, be able to)* refers to the physical ability to do something, while 可以 **kěyǐ** *(may, be permitted to)* refers to someone's having permission to do something.

可以 打电话吗？ Can I use your phone to make a phone call?
Kěyǐ dǎ diànhuà ma?
你不能 打电话。电话坏了。 You can't make a phone call. The phone is broken.
Nǐ bùnéng dǎ diànhuà. Diànhuà huài le.

The negative form of both 能 **néng** and 可以 **kěyǐ** is formed with 不 **bù**: 不能 **bùnéng** means *not able to* and 不可以 **bù kěyǐ** means *not permitted to*. Notice, however, that 能 **néng** and 可以 **kěyǐ** are often used more ambiguously in the dialogues in lesson 19. You see certain situations where 不能 打电话 **bùnéng dǎ diànhuà** and 不可以打电话 **bù kěyǐ dǎ diànhuà** are interchangeable.

The particle 了 le: a new situation

You have already learned that the aspect particle 了 **le**, following a verb, indicates that an action is complete.

了 **le** does not indicate past or present, but rather emphasizes that the action is finished.

In this lesson the aspect particle 了 **le** at the end of a sentence (or after an adjective) indicates a new or changed situation. 现在可以打扫我的房间了 **Xiànzài kěyǐ dǎsǎo wǒde fángjiān**

le *(You may clean my room now)* literally means now is the time that now you are permitted to clean up my room (but before this time you were not). 我的厕所坏了 **Wǒde cèsuǒ huài le** *(My toilet is broken)* means now there is something wrong with my toilet (but before it was working fine).

Measure words

Following the sentence structure below, ask for things using measure words.

Subject	Verb	Number	Measure word	Object
我 **Wǒ** I need a towel.	需要 **xūyào**	一 **yì**	条 **tiáo**	毛巾。 **máojīn.**
		一 **yí**	块 **kuài**	肥皂 **féizào**
		两 **liǎng**	个 **ge**	衣架 **yījià**
		一 **yì**	瓶 **píng**	水 **shuǐ**
		三 **sān**	个 **ge**	杯子 **bēizi**
		一 **yì**	卷 **juǎn**	卫生纸 **wèishēngzhǐ**
		一 **yì**	条 **tiáo**	床单 **chuángdān**
		一 **yí**	个 **ge**	房间 **fángjiān**
		一 **yí**	个 **ge**	灯 **dēng**

Which room are you in?

你住哪个房间 **Nǐ zhù nǐ ge fángjiān?** *(Which room are you in?)* is a very common question that a hotel attendant will ask when you request something to be sent to your room.

Question				Answer		
Subject	*Verb*	*Int.*	*Object*	*Subject*	*Verb*	*Object*
你	住	哪个	房间？	我	住	405 号房间。
Nǐ	**zhù**	**nǎ ge**	**fángjiān?**	**Wǒ**	**zhù**	**sì lǐng wǔ hào fángjiān.**
Which room are you in?				I am staying in room 405.		

Practice asking and answering questions with this pattern:

Question				Answer		
Subject	*Verb*	*Int.*	*Object*	*Subject*	*Verb*	*Object*
		多少号 **duōshao hào**				214
		多少号 **duōshao hào**	房间 **fángjiān**			321
		哪儿 **nǎr**				533
		哪个房间 **nǎ ge fángjiān**				这个房间 **zhè ge fángjiān**

To/from

Practice using the pattern of verb + simple complement, with 来 **lái** showing the action coming toward the speaker, and 去 **qù** showing the action going away from the speaker:

Subject	Verb	Object	Subject	Prep-phrase	Verb + qù/lái
我 **Wǒ**	要 **yào**	两个衣架。 **liǎng ge yījià.**	我 **Wǒ**	给你 **gěi nǐ**	送去/送来。 **sòng qù/sòng lái.**
I need two hangers.			I will send them to you.		
		一条毛巾 **yì tiáo máojīn**			送来 **sòng lái**

还要		三块肥皂 sān kuài féizào	送去 sòng qù
		两个杯子 **liǎng ge bēizi**	送去 **sòng qù**
hái	**yào**	卫生纸 **wèishēngzhǐ**	送来 **sòng lái**
		电话卡 **diànhuàkǎ**	买去 **mǎi qù**
		人民币 **Rénmínbì**	换去 **huàn qù**

Soon

Practice using 一会儿 **yí huìr** to mean *to do something soon, in a while*:

Subject	Verb	yí huìr	Other elements
我等 **Wǒ**	一会儿 **děng**	送 去。 **yí huìr**	 **sòng qu**
I will send (it) to you soon.			
	去 **qù**	一会儿 **yí huìr**	
	看 **kàn**	一会儿 **yí huìr**	书 **shū**
请 **Qǐng**	等 **děng**	一会儿 **yí huìr**	打扫我的房间 **dǎsǎo wǒde fángjiān**
	等 **děng**	一会儿 **yí huìr**	再来 **zài lái**
	坐 **zuò**	一会儿 **yí huìr**	

To be able to

Practice asking and answering questions with 能 **néng** *(can, be able to)* followed by a verb.

Subject	Aux	Verb	Object
我 **Wǒ**	能不能 **néng bùnéng**	打扫 **dǎsǎo**	房间？ **fángjiān?**
May I clean the room?			

Answer with 能 **néng** or 不能 **bùnéng**.

Subject	Aux	Verb	Object
		换 **huàn**	美元 **Měiyuán**
		修 **xiū**	灯 **dēng**
		买 **mǎi**	电话卡 **diànhuàkǎ**
		换 **huàn**	床单 **chuángdān**
		修 **xiū**	厕所 **cèsuǒ**

To be permitted

Practice asking and answering questions with 可以 **kěyǐ** *(may, can, be permitted to)* followed by a verb. Remember that the time word 现在 **xiànzài** must be placed either at the very beginning of a sentence or right after the subject and before the verb. It never comes at the end of a sentence.

"Now"	Subj.	Aux	Verb	Object	ma
现在 **Xiànzài**	我 **wǒ**	可以 **kěyǐ**	打 **dǎ**	电话 **diànhuà**	吗？ **ma?**

May I make phone calls now?

Answer with 可以 **kěyǐ** or 不可以 **bù kěyǐ**.

Practice this sentence structure using the verbs and objects provided:

			用 **yòng**	你的电话 **nǐde diànhuà**	
			去 **qù**	银行 **yínháng**	
			吃 **chī**	饭 **fàn**	
			找 **zhǎo**	马小姐 **Mǎ xiǎojie**	

To be broken

坏了 **huài le** *(to have become out of order* or *broken)* is a very useful expression for telling a hotel attendant that something is broken in your room and needs to be fixed.

Practice using this expression with the aspect particle 了 **le** following a verb to indicate a new or changed situation.

Topic	Verb	Particle
电话	坏	了。
Diànhuà	**huài**	**le.**

The telephone is broken.

厕所
cèsuǒ
杯子
bēizi
灯
dēng
床
chuáng
菜 (Here 坏 **huài** means *bad*, *rotten*)
cài

Pronunciation Note: Vowels "ü" and "u"

The Chinese vowel "ü" has no equivalent in English. The lips are rounded when pronouncing both "ü" and "u", but the tongue has different positions. To pronounce "ü", place the tip of your tongue against the back of the lower teeth. But to pronounce "u", keep your tongue away from the teeth, with the tip not touching any part of your mouth. Practice this by first rounding your lips and keeping your tongue in the back of your mouth to pronounce "u". Then without changing the position of your lips, slowly move your tongue from the back to the front, so that it touches your teeth, and pronounce "ü". Pronounce "u" and "ü" several times, one after the other, to feel the difference in position. Notice that Pinyin omits the umlaut except after "l" and "n". Try these examples:

Pinyin	Chinese	English
1. lù [as in English "Luke"]	路	road
2. lǚ [no English equivalent]	绿	green
3. nú [no English equivalent]	奴	slave
4. nǚ [no English equivalent]	女	woman

Pronunciation Practice

Read the following words aloud. Say the sounds carefully and listen for the difference between "ü" and "u".

"ü" (when following "y" or "j", the "ü" is written without the umlaut but still pronounced the same):

Pinyin	Characters	English
1. yú (yú)	鱼	fish
2. nǚ háizi (nǚ)	女孩子	girl
3. jūnduì (jūn)	军队	troops

"u" without umlaut, pronounced like the English "Luke":

Pinyin	Characters	English
4. rúguǒ	如果	if
5. nǔlì	努力	work hard
6. dùzi	肚子	stomach
7. zhǔnbèi	准备	to prepare

Read the following words aloud and pay special attention to the difference between "ü" and "u".

Pinyin	Characters	English
1. **dìtú**	地图	map
2. **fùnǚ**	妇女	women
3. **lǚxíng**	旅行	travel
4. **chūqù**	出去	go out
5. **cù**	醋	vinegar
6. **lúzi**	炉子	stove

Each entry below has an initial sound and a final sound that combine to form complete words. Read the initial and the final sound, then read the full word. Check your pronunciation on the audio.

Group A:		Group B:		Group C:		Group D:	
g	**āi**	y	**áng**	d	**āi**	zh	**uāng**
k	**uài**	w	**ōng**	t	**uì**	ch	**í**
h	**uǎn**	ü	**ān**	l	**ún**	sh	**ùn**
				n	**uǎn**	r	**èn**

Read the following medical terms aloud.

1. **shēntǐ**	身体	body
2. **bízi**	鼻子	nose
3. **bèi**	背	back
4. **ěrduo**	耳朵	ear
5. **dùzi**	肚子	stomach
6. **gēbo**	胳膊	arm
7. **liǎn**	脸	face
8. **yāo**	腰	waist
9. **shétou**	舌头	tongue
10. **shǒu**	手	hand

11. **tóu**	头	head
12. **tuǐ**	腿	leg
13. **yǎnjīng**	眼睛	eye
14. **zhījia**	指甲	nail
15. **yá**	牙	teeth
16. **zhèngzhuàng**	症状	symptoms
17. **fāshāo**	发烧	fever
18. **fālěng**	发冷	chill
19. **fāyán**	发炎	infection
20. **gǎnmào**	感冒	cold
21. **guòmǐn**	过敏	allergy
22. **késou**	咳嗽	cough
23. **hūxī**	呼吸	breath
24. **tóuyūn**	头晕	dizzy
25. **tù**	吐	to throw up
26. **lā dùzi**	拉肚子	diarrhea
27. **liúbítì**	流鼻涕	runny nose
28. **liúxuè**	流血	bleeding
29. **shāoshāng**	烧伤	burn
30. **téng**	疼	hurt

Read the following hospital terms and doctor's instructions aloud.

1. **yīyuàn**	医院	hospital
2. **yīwùshì**	医务室	clinic
3. **guàhàochù**	挂号处	registration office
4. **nèikē**	内科	department of internal medicine
5. **wàikē**	外科	surgical department
6. **yákē**	牙科	department of dentistry
7. **jízhěnshì**	急诊室	emergency room
8. **qǔyàochù/ yàofáng**	取药处/药房	pharmacy
9. **huàyànshì**	化验室	laboratory
10. **X-guāng shì**	X光室	X-ray room

11. zhùshèshì	注射室	injection room
12. zhùyuànchù	住院处	admission office

Doctor's instructions:

13. Qǐng bǎ zuǐ zhāngkāi.	请把嘴张开·	Please open your mouth.
14. Qǐng bǎ shétou shēn chūlái.	请把舌头伸出来·	Please stick out your tongue.
15. Shēn hūxī.	深呼吸·	Take a deep breath.
16. Qǐng bǎ yīfu tuōdiào.	请把衣服脱掉·	Please take off your clothes.
17. Tǎngxià.	躺下	Lie down.
18. Zhàn qǐlái.	站起来·	Stand up.
19. Qǐng bǎ xiùzi juǎn qǐlái.	请把袖子卷起来·	Please roll up your sleeves.

day: 21

Checking Out

Day 21 is where you will practice what you have just learned in the previous two lessons. Make sure you listen to the audio when you see the CD symbol and answer the questions fully before continuing on to the next lesson. You can check your answers in the Key to Exercises at the back of the book.

CHECKING UP...

When checking out of a hotel, don't be alarmed when the staff go to check the room before processing check out – this is standard practice everywhere.

Exercises

Exercise 1

Listen to the compounds or phrases and write what you hear in Pinyin.

1. .... lì
2. .... shì
3. ....xíng
4. .... lì
5. ....xùn
6. .... shī
7. ....zi
8. ....zi
9. fǎ ....
10. mǎ ....
11. fù ....
12. mì ....
13. fèn ....
14. kǎo ....
15. bùjué ....

Exercise 2

Read and listen to the dialogue, and then answer the questions below.

First review these new vocabulary words:

zěnmeyàng 怎么样 (how)

búcuò 不错 (not bad)

liàng 亮 (bright)

gānjing 干净 (clean)

fúwùyuán 服务员 (attendant)

A: Male foreigner 男外宾 **nán wàibīn**;

B: Female foreigner 女外宾 **nǚ wàibīn**

A: 你住在几号房间？

B: 我住在302号房间？

A: 那个房间怎么样？

B: 那个房间不错，很亮，很干净。你住在几号？

A: 我住306号。那个房间不太好.

B: 怎么不好？

A: 那个房间没有毛巾，床单也不太干净.

B: 你告诉服务员了吗？

A: 告诉了他们说给我送毛巾来，也给我换床单.

Indicate whether the following statements are true or false.

1. **The room number of the female foreigner is 302.** True ( ) False ( )
2. **The male foreigner's room is in good condition.** True ( ) False ( )
3. **The female foreigner needs towels and clean sheets.** True ( ) False ( )
4. **The attendant will send towels and change the sheets.** True ( ) False ( )

Exercise 3

How many of the following things can you name in Chinese? Write the names in Pinyin in the blanks.

1. **towels** ....
2. **soap** ....
3. **toilet paper** ....
4. **hanger** ....

Exercise 4

To prepare for your stay in a hotel in China, translate the following sentences into Chinese. Write the Chinese in Pinyin or characters.

1. **I need one roll of toilet paper and three hangers.** ....

   ....

   ....

2. **My lamp is broken.** ....

   ....

   ....

3. **Who is it? Please come back later** . ...

   ....

   ....

4. **Please clean my room now. Could you change my sheets?** ....

   ....

   ....

5. Please send one bar of soap and two towels to my room. I am staying in room 312.

Thanks. ....

....

....

day:22

Getting Lost

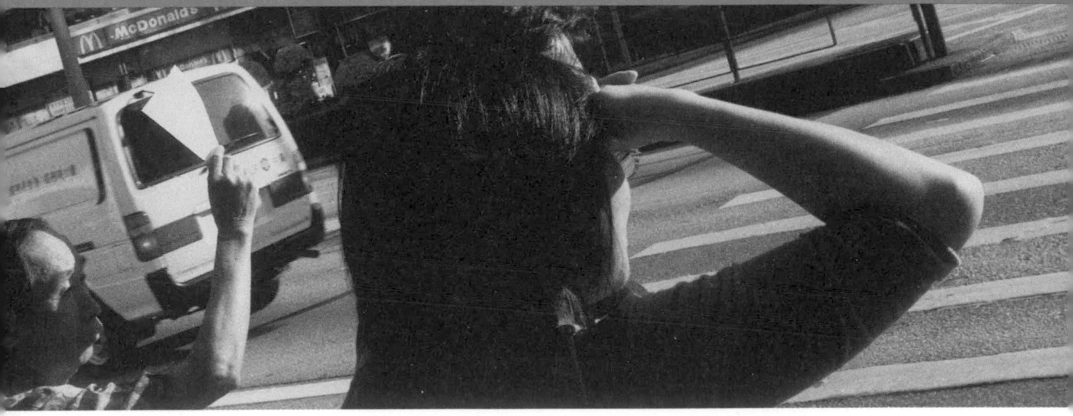

Day 22 takes you out and about exploring. You will learn how to ask for directions and you will be able to listen to sample dialogues with native speakers to help you to improve your comprehension and listening skills.

STREET NAMES AND DIRECTIONS

*Street names in China often include the words **east, west, north,** or **south.** For example, 天安门西大街 **Tiānānmén Xīdàjiē** literally means **Tiānānmén West Boulevard,** which tells you that the boulevard is west of **Tiānānmén Square.** Those directional words with a street name can help you find your way more easily.*

Vocabulary

Key Expressions

请问，大门在哪儿？
Qǐng wèn, dàmén zài nǎr?
Excuse me, where is the gate?

英文系怎么走？
Yīngwénxì zěnme zǒu?
How can I get to the English Department?

一直走
yìzhí zǒu
go straight

左转 / 右转
zuǒ zhuǎn/yòu zhuǎn
turn left/turn right

附近有网吧吗？
Fùjìn yǒu wǎngbā ma?
Is there an Internet cafe nearby?

New Words I • 生词一

Characters	Pinyin	English
饭馆(儿)	**fànguǎn(r)**	*restaurant*
英文	**Yīngwén**	*English language*
系	**xì**	*department (in a college)*
英文系	**Yīngwénxì**	*English Department*
前	**qián**	*front; forward, in front of; preceding*
前边	**qiánbian**	*in front, ahead*
走	**zǒu**	*to walk, to go, to leave*
一直	**yìzhí**	*straight, straight on, continuously*
经过	**jīngguò**	*to pass by, to pass through*
大门	**dàmén**	*main entrance*
大	**dà**	*big, large, major, old* (when referring to age)
门	**mén**	*entrance, door, gate*

往	**wǎng/wàng**	*to go; toward, in the direction of*
右	**yòu**	*right; right-hand*
转	**zhuǎn/ zhùan**	*to turn, to change, to rotate*
中文	**Zhōngwén**	*Chinese language*
中文系	**Zhōngwénxì**	*Chinese Deparment*
旁边	**pángbian**	*side; beside, nearby*
外教	**wàijiào**	*foreign teacher* (short form of 外国教师 **wàiguó jiàoshī**)
吧	**ba**	(used to make a mild imperative sentence, to imply agreement or a degree of certainty, to express unwillingness or hesitation)
教	**jiāo/jiào**	*to teach*
英语	**Yīngyǔ**	*English language*
附近	**fùjìn**	*nearby; in the vicinity of, closely*
网吧	**wǎngbā**	*Internet cafe*
右边	**yòubian**	*right side*
教学楼	**jiàoxuélóu**	*classroom building*
学	**xué**	*to study, to learn; school, knowledge*
图书馆	**túshūguǎn**	*library*
中间	**zhōngjiān**	*middle, center; in between*

Dialogue I • 对话一

Roles

A: Foreigner — 外国人 **wàiguórén;**
B: Chinese person — 中国人 **Zhōngguórén**

A:	请问，英文系在 哪儿？	**Qǐng wèn, Yīngwénxì zài nǎr?**
B:	在前边。	**Zài qiánbian.**
A:	怎么走？	**Zěnme zǒu?**
B:	一直走，经过大门，往右转，在中文系旁边。	**Yìzhí zǒu, jīngguò dàmén, wàng yòu zhuǎn, zài Zhōngwénxì pángbian.**
	您是外教吧？	**Nín shì wàijiào ba?**
A:	是，我在英文系教英语。请问，附近有网吧吗？	**Shì, wǒ zài Yīngwénxì jiāo Yīngyǔ. Qǐng wèn, fùjìn yǒu wǎngbā ma?**
B:	有，在大门右边，教学楼和图书馆的中间。	**Yǒu, zài dàmén yòubian, jiàoxuélóu hé túshūguǎn de zhōngjiān.**

Translation of Dialogue I

A: Excuse me, where is the English Department?
B: Up ahead.
A: How do I get there?
B: Go straight, pass the main gate and turn right. It is next to the Chinese Department. Are you a foreign teacher?
A: Yes, I teach English at the English Department. May I ask, is there an Internet cafe nearby?
B: Yes, there is one to the right of the main gate, between the classroom building and the library.

New Words II • 生词二

Characters	Pinyin	English
马路	**mǎlù**	*road, street*
对面	**duìmiàn**	*on the opposite side, across the street*
过	**guò**	*to pass, to cross, to celebrate, to spend (time), to go through*
远	**yuǎn**	*far away, distant*

左	**zuǒ**	*left; left-hand*
左边	**zuǒbian**	*left side*
书店	**shūdiàn**	*bookstore*
后	**hòu**	*rear, back; behind, after*
后边	**hòubian**	*back, rear*
大学	**dàxué**	*university, college*
办公室	**bàngōngshì**	*office*
外事处	**wàishìchù**	*Foreign Affairs Office*
商学院	**shāngxué-yuàn**	*Business School*
法学院	**fǎxuéyuàn**	*Law School*
留学生	**liúxuéshēng**	*student studying abroad, foreign student*
宿舍	**sùshè**	*dorm*
医院	**yīyuàn**	*hospital*
北京	**Běijīng**	*Beijing*
汽车站	**qìchēzhàn**	*bus stop*

Dialogue II • 对话二

Roles

A: American 美国人 **Měiguórén**;
B: Chinese person 中国人 **Zhōngguórén**

A: 请 问，哪儿有厕所？ **Qǐng wèn, nǎr yǒu cèsuǒ?**

B: 厕所在马路对面，过了马路往右走。 **Cèsuǒ zài mǎlù duìmiàn, guò le mǎlù wàng yòu zǒu.**

A: 远吗？ **Yuǎn ma?**

B: 不远。 **Bù yuǎn.**

A: 怎么走？ **Zěnme zǒu?**

B: 往前走，经过中国银行，银行的左边是书店， 书店的后边有一个厕所。 **Wàng qián zǒu, jīngguò Zhōngguó Yínháng, yínháng de zuǒbian shì shūdiàn, shūdiàn de hòubian yǒu yí ge cèsuǒ.**

Translation of Dialogue II

A: Excuse me, where is the restroom/public toilet?
B: It is on the other side of the street. Turn right after crossing the street.
A: Is it far?
B: It is not far.
A: How can I get there?
B: Walk straight ahead, and go past the Bank of China. To the left of the bank is a bookstore. The toilet is behind the bookstore.

day:23

Out & About

Day 23 explores the grammatical aspects of prepositions in Chinese. Take the time to do the pronunciaiton practice and to understand the different elements of this chapter.

CITY DISTRICTS

Cities in China are divided into districts. When you want to find a place in a city, you first need to find out which district it is in so you will know its general area. 北京 ***Běijīng*** *has fourteen districts, of which* 西城 ***Xīchéng****,* 东城 ***Dōngchén****, and* 宣武 ***Xuānwǔ*** *districts make up the downtown area. Most foreign embassies and company offices are in the* 朝阳 ***Cháoyáng*** *district. Most universities, including Beijing University, are located in the* 海淀 ***Hǎidiàn*** *district.*

Grammar

在 zài (to be in/at)

在 **zài** *(to be in/at)* can be a preposition or a verb. 在 **zài** is a verb in the sentence 英文系在哪儿？ **Yīngwénxì zài nǎr?** *(Where is the English Department?)*. In this sentence, 在 **zài** is followed by the interrogative pronoun 哪 儿 **nǎr** *(where)*. The answer is formed by replacing the interrogative pronoun 哪儿 **nǎr** with a noun of place, in this case 前边 **qiánbian** *(front side)*. Here are some examples of 在 **zài** as a verb:

银行 在前边。 **Yínháng zài qiánbian.**	The bank is in the front.
马小姐在吗？ **Mǎ xiǎojie zài ma?**	Is Miss Ma in?

You can identify 在 **zài** as a preposition, rather than a verb, when there is a main verb in the sentence and when 在 **zài** is followed by a place word: 在 **zài** + place word + verb. Here are some examples of 在 **zài** as a preposition:

我 在 食堂 吃 饭。 **Wǒ zài shítáng chīfàn.**	I eat in the cafeteria.
他 在 银行换 钱。 **Tā zài yínháng huàn qián.**	He exchanges money at the bank.

Sentences with subjects omitted

Adverbs (and adverbial phrases) are placed before the verb in a sentence. Examples are:

怎么 **zěnme** (how)	*in*	怎么走？ **Zěnme zǒu?** (How do I get there?)
一直 **yìzhí** (straight)	*in*	一直走 **yìzhí zǒu** (go straight)
往前 **wàng qián** (go forward)	*in*	往前走 **wàng qián zǒu** (walk forward)
左 **zuǒ** (left)	*in*	左转 **zuǒ zhuǎn** (turn left)

Notice that the Chinese word order is different from English word order. In Chinese an adverb always precedes the verb; in English it may follow a verb.

Left turn / Right turn

右转 **yòu zhuǎn** *(turn right)*, 左转 **zuǒ zhuǎn** *(turn left)*, 左走 **zuǒ zǒu** *(walk towards the left)* and 右走 **yòu zǒu (walk towards the right)** are colloquial expressions that omit the preposition 向 **xiàng** *(towards)* or 往 **wàng** *(to, towards)*.

The full form of 右转 **yòu zhuǎn** *(turn right)* is 向右转 **xiàng yòu zhuǎn** or 往右转 **wàng yòu zhuǎn** *(turn towards the right)*; 左 **zuǒ** and 右 **yòu** are position words. 向右 **xiàng yòu** and 往右 **wàng yòu** are prepositional phrases modifying the verb 转 **zhuǎn** *(to turn)*.

在 zài, 有 yǒu and 是 shì (is, are)

Three verbs are used to describe a location:

a. 在 **zài** (to be in, to be at)

b. 是 **shì** (is, are)

c. 有 **yǒu** (there is/are)

a. To use 在 **zài** to tell the location of a place:

[target place] 在 **zài** [location]

The target place is the place someone is looking for, such as 英文系 **Yīngwénxì** (Department of English). The location is new information for the listener, and tells where the target place is.

With the verb 在 **zài**, the target place must come first, as the subject of the sentence. Then comes the verb 在 **zài**, followed by the location:

厕所在马路对面。 **Cèsuǒ zài mǎlù duìmiàn.**	The toilet is on the other side of the street.
教学楼在 英文系右边。 **Jiàoxuélóu zài Yīngwénxì yòubian.**	The classroom building is to the right of the English Department.

b. You can also use the verb 是 **shì** *(is/are)* to tell the location of a place.

[location] 是 **shì** [target place]

With the verb 是 **shì**, the location must come first as the subject of the sentence. Then comes the verb 是 **shì**, followed by the target place:

银 行的 左边是书 店。 **Yínháng de zuǒbian shì shūdiàn.**	On the left side of the bank is the bookstore.

马路 的 对面是厕所。 Across the street is the toilet.
Mǎlù de duìmiàn shì cèsuǒ.

c. The third choice is to use 有 **yǒu** *(to exist, there is/are)* to give information about the location of a place.

[location] 有**yǒu** (一个 **yí ge**) + [target place]

The sentence pattern containing the verb 有 **yǒu** is the same as the pattern containing 是 **shì**, except that the target place usually is an indefinite noun preceded by the measure word 一个 **yí ge** *(one, a)*.

大 门 旁边 有 一 个 网吧。 There is an Internet cafe next to the main gate.
Dàmén pángbian yǒu yí ge wǎngbā.

马路 对面 有 一 个 厕所。 There is a toilet on the other side of the street.
Mǎlù duìmiàn yǒu yí ge cèsuǒ.

A street intersection in Beijing

Asking locations with 在 zài

To ask for the location of a place with the phrase *Excuse me, where is . . . ?*, use the following pattern, with 在 **zài** *(to be in/at)* used as a verb:

请问 **Qǐng wèn** + location of a place + 在哪儿 **zài nǎr**?

The pattern for the answer is:

Target place	Verb	Location
英文系 **Yīngwénxì**	在 **zài**	前边。 **qiánbian.**

The English Department is straight ahead.

Practice asking and answering questions about the location of a place using the target places and locations provided:

外事处 **wàishìchù**	大门旁边 **dàmén pángbian**
网吧 **wǎngbā**	马路对面 **mǎlù duìmiàn**
教学楼 **jiàoxuélóu**	那边 **nàbian**
大门 **dàmén**	左边 **zuǒbian**
中文系 **Zhōngwénxì**	商学院后边 **shāngxuéyuàn hòubian**
法学院 **Fǎxuéyuàn**	英文系旁边 **Yīngwénxì pángbian**

Asking for directions

A frequently used pattern for asking directions is:

请问 **Qǐng wèn** + target place + 怎么走 **zěnme zǒu**? *Excuse me, how do I get to . . . ?*

The pattern for answering this question is:

往 **Wàng** + direction + verb

Practice asking for directions using the words for target place, below. Notice that the verb comes at the end of the sentence, after the adverb (and adverbial phrase) that modifies it.

Question				Answer		
请问，	网吧	怎么	走？	往	前	走。
Qǐng wèn,	**wǎngbā**	**zěnme**	**zǒu?**	**Wàng**	**qián**	**zǒu.**
How can I get to the Internet cafe?				Go straight ahead.		

北京宾馆
Beijing Bīnguǎn
银行
yínháng
汽车站
qìchēzhàn
医院
yīyuàn
书店
shūdiàn

Giving directions

Practice giving directions with 转 **zhuǎn** *(to turn)* and a direction word, which comes before 转 **zhuǎn**. Notice that this is the opposite of English word order (turn left, turn right, turn back).

Direction	Turn
左	转。
zuǒ	**zhuǎn.**
Turn left.	
右	转。
yòu	**zhuǎn.**
Turn right.	
后	转。
hòu	**zhuǎn.**
Turn back	

Practice adding 往 **wàng** *(to, toward, in the direction of)* to this phrase.

Toward	Direction	Turn
往 **Wàng**	左 **zuǒ**	转。 **zhuǎn.**

Turn (towards the) left.

	右 **yòu**	
	后 **hòu**	
	北 **běi**	
	南 **nán**	
	东 **dōng**	
	西 **xī**	

Directions with 在 zài

Practice using 在 **zài** *(be in/at)* as a verb to tell directions.

The target place (the place someone is looking for) comes first, as the subject of the sentence. Then comes the verb 在 **zài**, followed by the location.

图书馆 **Túshūguǎn**	在 **zài**	前边。 **qiánbian.**

The library is straight ahead.

Practice forming sentences in this structure, using the following locations and target places.

Location	Target Place
宾馆 **bīnguǎn**	马路对面 **mǎlù duìmiàn**
中国银行 **Zhōngguó Yínháng**	左边 **zuǒbian**

厕所 **cèsuǒ**	大门 右边 **dàmén yòubian**
医院 **yīyuàn**	那边 **nàbian**
网吧 **wǎngbā**	商店旁边 **shāngdiàn pángbian**
电话 **diànhuà**	教学楼旁边 **jiàoxuélóu pángbian**
食堂 **shítáng**	后边 **hòubian**
汽车站 **qìchēzhàn**	左边 **zuǒbian**
医院 **yīyuàn**	宾馆右边 **bīnguǎn yòubian**

Directions with 是 shì

When the verb 是 **shì** *(is/are)* is used to tell the location of a place, the location comes first, as the subject of the sentence. Then comes the verb 是 **shì**, followed by the target place.

银行的左边 **Yínháng de zuǒ biān**	是 **shì**	书店。 **shūdiàn.**

On the left side of the bank is the bookstore.

Practice forming sentences in this structure, using the following locations and target places.

Location	Target Place
书店的旁边 **shūdiàn de pángbian**	商店 **shāngdiàn**
那边 **nàbian**	宾馆 **bīnguǎn**
教学楼的前边 **jiàoxuélóu de qiánbian**	食堂 **shítáng**
商店的后边 **shāngdiàn de hòubian**	邮局 **yóujú**
饭馆的右边 **fànguǎn de yòubian**	银行 **yínháng**

大门的左边 **dàmén de zuǒbian**	网吧 **wǎngbā**
马路的对面 **mǎlù de duìmiàn**	厕所 **cèsuǒ**

Directions with 有 yǒu

Practice using the verb 有 **yǒu** *(there is/are)* to tell the location of a place.

The sentence pattern with 有 **yǒu** is the same as with 是 **shì**, but the target place usually is an indefinite noun preceded by the measure word 一个 **yí ge** *(one, a)*.

教学楼 的旁边 **Jiàoxuélóu de pángbian**	有 **yǒu**	一个 **yí ge**	书店。 **shūdiàn.**

Next to the classroom building is a bookstore.

Practice forming sentences in this structure, using the words the following locations and target places.

Location	Target Place
前边 **qiánbian**	厕所 **cèsuǒ**
宾馆的旁边 **bīnguǎn de pángbian**	饭馆 **fànguǎn**
大门的右边 **dàmén de yòubian**	网吧 **wǎngbā**
银行的后边 **yínháng de hòubian**	邮局 **yóujú**
饭馆的对面 **fànguǎn de duìmiàn**	电话 **diànhuà**
法学院的旁边 **Fǎxuéyuàn de pángbian**	商学院 **shāngxuéyuàn**
那边 **nàbian**	医院 **yīyuàn**
马路对面 **Mǎlù duìmiàn**	中国银行 **Zhōngguó Yínháng**

Pronunciation Note: The final "i"

In Pinyin the letter "i" represents three different vowel sounds, depending on which initial it follows.

Following most initials, the pronunciation of "i" resembles the English sound "ee".

Pinyin	Chinese	English
1. **yī**	一	one
2. **qī**	七	seven
3. **dìdi**	弟弟	younger brother
4. **chūnjié**	春节	Spring Festival
5. **jīng**	京	capital
6. **jī**	机	machine

Notice that in Chinese "i" is never pronounced as the English long vowel "i" (as in "right").

When "i" follows the initials "z", "c", or "s", it is pronounced as just an extension of the "z", "c", or "s", while the tip of your tongue stays against the back of lower teeth, and with vibration of the vocal cords.

Pinyin	Chinese	English
1. **zì**	字	character, word
2. **cí**	词	word, term
3. **sī**	丝	silk

When "i" follows the initials "zh", "ch", "sh", or "r" it is pronounced something like "r" and as just an extension of the "zh", "ch", "sh", or "r" with vibration of the vocal cords. With "zhi", "chi", or "shi" the tip of your tongue pulls back slightly from the roof of your mouth, but with "ri" the tongue does not move.

Pinyin	Chinese	English
1. **zhīdao**	知道	to know
2. **chīfàn**	吃饭	to eat a meal
3. **lǎoshī**	老师	teacher
4. **jiérì**	节日	holiday

Pronunciation Practice

Say the following words or phrases aloud, paying particular attention to pronunciation of the vowel "i."

Pinyin	Characters	English
1. **Yīngwénxì**	英文系	English Department
2. **zìzhìqū**	自治区	autonomous region
3. **zìxí**	自习	study by self in scheduled time or free time
4. **mínǐ**	迷你	mini (miniskirt)
5. **chídào**	迟到	to be late, to arrive late
6. **háizi**	孩子	child
7. **sīchóu**	丝绸	silk
8. **sìshēng**	四声	four tones
9. **Rìběn**	日本	Japan
10. **cíqì**	瓷器	porcelain
11. **zhīshi**	知识	knowledge
12. **chǐzi**	尺子	ruler
13. **shīzi**	狮子	lion

Each entry below has an initial sound and a final sound that combine to form complete words. Read the initial sound and the final sound, then read the full word. Check your pronunciation on the audio.

Group A:		Group B:		Group C:		Group D:	
b	**ēn**	zh	**èi**	j	**uān**	z	**òng**
p	**éng**	ch	**āo**	q	**ū**	c	**èng**
m	**ián**	sh	**éi**	x	**uē**	s	**uì**
f	**ǎng**	r	**ǎng**				

Practice Pinyin by reading the following terms aloud.

1. **diànnǎo** 电脑 computer
2. **diàndēngpào** 电灯泡 light bulb
3. **chāzuò** 插座 socket
4. **diàndēng** 电灯 light

5. **diànchí** 电池 battery
6. **yī hào diànchí** 一号电池 D size battery
7. **èr hào diànchí** 二号电池 C size battery
8. **wǔ hào diànchí** 五号电池 AA size battery
9. **qī hào diànchí** 七号电池 AAA size battery
10. **shōuyīnjī** 收音机 radio
11. **shǒujī** 手机 cell phone
12. **hūjī** 呼机 beeper
13. **CD-pán** CD-盘 / **jīguāng chàngpán** 激光唱盘 compact disc
14. **lùyīndài** 录音带 cassette tape
15. **lùyīnjī** 录音机 tape recorder
16. **lùxiàngjī** 录象机 video recorder

day: 24

Finding your Way

Day 24 is about practicing what you have learned so far. There was lots to learn in the last chapter so take the time to go back over anything you are ensure of to help you go through the exercises.

CITY DISTRICTS…

*深圳 **Shēnzhèn** is divided into six districts: 罗湖 **Luóhú**, 福田 **Fútián**, 盐田 **Yántián**, 南山 **Nánshān**, 龙岗 **Lónggǎng** and 保安 **Bǎo'ān**. **Luóhú** district is the downtown area of the city.*

Exercises

Exercise 1

Listen to the words and phrases on the CD, then write the correct Pinyin spelling with tone marks in the blanks below.

1. ....

....

2. ....

....

3. ....

....

4. ....

....

5. ....

....

6. ....

....

7. ....

....

8. ....

....

9. ....

....

10. ....

....

Exercise 2

Read and listen to the dialogue, and then answer the questions below.

First review these new vocabulary words:

图书馆 **túshūguǎn** (library)

从 **cóng** (from)

就 **jiù** (just)

电影院 **diànyǐngyuàn** (movie theater)

对 **duì** (correct)

A: English person 英国人 **Yīngguórén;**

B: Chinese person 中国人 **Zhōngguórén**

A: 请问图书馆在哪儿？

B: 哪个图书馆？是大图书馆吗？

A: 是。我要去大图书馆。

B: 你从这儿一直走，左边有一个电影院，过了电影院，就是大图书馆。大图书馆在左边。

A: 我从这儿一直走，过了电影院，左边就是大图书馆，对吗？

B: 对。

A: 好。谢谢!

B: 不谢!

Questions:

1. What does the English person want? ....

....

....

2. What is the English person looking for? ....

....

....

3. **On which side of the library is the movie theater?** ....

....

....

Exercise 3

Change the following sentences into questions using the word in the parenthesis.

Examples:

大门对面有网吧。 (在) → 网吧在大门 对面。

Dàmén duìmiàn yǒu wǎngbā. Zài Wǎngbā zài Dàmén duìmiàn.

1. 商店旁边是书店。 (有)

   Shāngdiàn pángbian shì shūdiàn. yǒu

....

2. 英文系在教学楼旁边。 (是)

   Yīngwénxì zài jiàoxuélóu pángbian. shì

....

3. 银行旁边是邮局。 (在)

   Yínháng pángbian shì yóujú. zài

....

4. 食堂在七号楼旁边。 (是)

   Shítáng zài qīhàolóu pángbian. shì

....

5. 马路对面是中国银行。 (有)

   Mǎlù duìmiàn shì Zhōngguó Yínháng. yǒu

....

6. 书店后面有一个厕所。 (在)

Shūdiàn hòumiàn yǒu yí ge cèsuǒ. zài

....

Exercise 4

To prepare for a trip to China, translate the following sentences into Chinese. Write the Chinese in Pinyin or characters.

1. **Where is the bathroom?** ....

....

....

....

2. **Where is the English Department? It is behind the classroom building.** ....

....

....

....

3. **How can I get to the Bank of China? Go straight, and then turn left.** ....

....

....

....

4. **Is there an Internet cafe around here? The Internet cafe is on the left side of the gate.** ....

....

....

....

5. Is it far? How can I get there? ....

....

....

....

6. Excuse me, where is the bookstore? First go straight, pass the Bank of China, and then turn left. ....

....

....

7. Is the hospital across the street from the main gate? ....

....

....

....

8. The post office is not far. ....

....

....

....

day: 25

Time

Day 25 is all about learning how to tell the time. You will learn the vocabulary you need for this and learn new words to express daily activities. You will also learn how to say you want/will. Listen to the dialogues by native speakers - by now they should be easier to understand.

12 AND 24-HOUR TIME SYSTEMS

In China the 24-hour clock is used by the media, business and government, as well as for all official schedules, such as train and airplane times. In daily conversation, however, people usually use the 12-hour clock, and add ***morning, afternoon*** *or* ***evening: shàngwǔ qī diǎn*** *(7:00 in the morning),* ***xiàwǔ sì diǎn*** *(4:00 in the afternoon), or* ***wǎnshàng jiǔ diǎn*** *(9:00 in the evening).*

Vocabulary

Key Expressions

现在几点？ **Xiànzài jǐ diǎn?**	*What time is it now?*
下午你有课吗？ **Xiàwǔ nǐ yǒu kè ma?**	*Do you have class in the afternoon?*
一起去…，好吗？ **Yìqǐ qù…, hǎo ma?**	*Shall we go to … together?*
…你常常做什么？ **…nǐ chángcháng zuò shénme?**	*What do you often do in …?*

New Words I • 生词一

Characters	Pinyin	English
几	**jǐ**	*how many; a few, several*
点	**diǎn**	*o'clock; (decimal) point; to choose, to mark*
几点	**jǐ diǎn**	*What time?*
差	**chà**	*short of, wanting; to differ from*
吧	**bā**	*bar, cafe*
吧	**ba**	(used to make a mild imperative, to imply agreement or a degree of certainty, to express unwillingness or hesitation)
上	**shàng**	*first, upper; to go up, to get on*
上午	**shàngwǔ**	*morning, a.m.*
午	**wǔ**	*noon*
半	**bàn**	*half, partly*
课	**kè**	*class, course*

上课	**shàngkè**	*to go to class, to teach a class*
汉语	**Hànyǔ**	*Chinese language*
下午	**xiàwǔ**	*afternoon*
下课	**xiàkè**	*class is over; to dismiss class*
刻	**kè**	*quarter of an hour, 15 minutes*
一刻	**yí kè**	*one quarter of an hour, 15 minutes*
三刻	**sān kè**	*three quarters of an hour, 45 minutes*
以后	**yǐhòu**	*after; later on, afterwards;*
一起	**yìqǐ**	*together*
好吗	**hǎo ma**	*Is it OK? Shall we?*
好吧	**hǎo ba**	*OK, all right*
见	**jiàn**	*to meet, to see, to call on*

Dialogue I • 对话一

Roles

A:	Chinese person	中国人 **Zhōngguórén;**
B:	French person	法国人 **Fǎguórén**

A:	现在几点？	**Xiànzài jǐ diǎn?**
B:	现在差十分八点。	**Xiànzài chà shí fēn bā diǎn.**
A:	我上午八点半要上汉语课。	**Wǒ shàngwǔ bā diǎn bàn yào shàng Hànyǔkè.**
B:	下午你有课吗？	**Xiàwǔ nǐ yǒu kè ma?**
A:	我下午有英语课。	**Wǒ xiàwǔ yǒu Yīngyǔkè.**
B:	你几点下课？	**Nǐ jǐ diǎn xiàkè?**
A:	四点一刻。	**Sì diǎn yí kè.**
B:	下课以后我们一起去网吧好吗？	**Xiàkè yǐhòu wǒmen yìqǐ qù wǎngbā, hǎo ma?**
A:	好吧，几点见？	**Hǎo ba, jǐ diǎn jiàn?**
B:	五点五分我去找你。	**Wǔ diǎn wǔ fēn wǒ qù zhǎo nǐ.**

Translation of Dialogue I

A: What time is it now?
B: Ten to eight.
A: I have Chinese class at 8:30 in the morning.
B: Do you have class in the afternoon?
A: I have English class in the afternoon.
B: When is your class over?
A: 4:15.
B: Shall we go to the Internet cafe together after your class?
A: OK. When shall we meet?
B: I will go to find you at 5:05.

要 yào (to want; will)

You have already learned the use of the verb 要 **yào** as *to want*:

我要一 张IP卡 **Wǒ yào yì zhāng IP kǎ.**	I want to buy an IP phone card.

But 要 **yào** can also be an auxiliary verb that comes before the main verb and means *going to* or *will*, indicating that an action or event will occur in the future:

我八点半要上汉语课。 I will go to Chinese class at 8:30.
Wǒ bā diǎn bàn yào shàng Hànyǔkè.

上课 shàngkè and 课 kè

上课 **shàngkè** can mean *to go to class/to attend a class* as in:

我八点半要上课。 At 8:30 I will go to (attend or teach) class.
Wǒ bā diǎn bàn yào shàngkè.

but 上课 **shàngkè** can also mean *to begin a class* as in:

现在上课。 Class is beginning now.
Xiànzài shàngkè.

In both of those instances 课 **kè** means class, but when you say 汉语课 **Hànyǔkè** *(Chinese language class)*, 课 **kè** means *course* or *subject*. 课 **kè** can also mean lesson, as in the chapter title 第九课 **dì jiǔ kè** *(Lesson Nine)*.

去 **qù** *(to go)* can be directly followed by a noun of place:

去食堂 to go to the cafeteria
qù shítáng
去网吧 to go to the Internet cafe
qù wǎngbā

Notice that the noun following 去 **qù** must be a place. If you want to use a person's name or a pronoun after 去 **qù**, you must add 这儿 **zhèr** or 那儿 **nàr** after the person's name or pronoun. For example:

去你那儿 go to your place
qù nǐ nàr

When 去 **qù** is followed by another verb, as in 去吃饭 **qù chīfàn**, it is like the English phrase *to go (to) eat*.

New Words II • 生词二

Characters	Pinyin	English
早上	**zǎoshang**	*morning*
起床	**qǐchuáng**	*to get up*
洗澡	**xǐzǎo**	*to take a shower, to take a bath*
早饭	**zǎofàn**	*breakfast*
上班	**shàngbān**	*to go to work, to go to the office*
中午	**zhōngwǔ**	*noon*
午饭	**wǔfàn**	*lunch*
下班	**xiàbān**	*to get out of work, to go off duty*
晚上	**wǎnshang**	*evening, night*
常常	**chángcháng**	*often*
做	**zuò**	*to do*
跟	**gēn**	*with*
朋友	**péngyou**	*friend*
睡觉	**shuìjiào**	*to go to bed, to sleep*
有时候	**yǒu shíhòu**	*sometimes, at times*
以前	**yǐqián**	*prior to, ago, before*
晚饭	**wǎnfàn**	*dinner*
休息	**xiūxi**	*to rest*
睡午觉	**shuì wǔjiào**	*to take a noon-time nap*

Dialogue II • 对话二

Roles

A: 你早上几点起床？ **Nǐ zǎoshang jǐ diǎn qǐchuáng?**

B: 七点。起床以后我先洗澡，再去吃早饭。我九点上班。 **Qī diǎn. Qǐchuáng yǐhòu wǒ xiān xǐzǎo, zài qù chī zǎofàn. Wǒ jiǔ diǎn shàngbān.**

A: 你中午几点去食堂？ **Nǐ zhōngwǔ jǐ diǎn qù shítáng?**

B: 十二点我去吃午饭。 **Shí'èr diǎn wǒ qù chī wǔfàn.**

A: 你几点下班？ **Nǐ jǐdiǎn xiàbān?**

B: 我五点下班。 **Wǒ wǔ diǎn xiàbān.**

A: 晚上你常常做什么？ **Wǎnshang nǐ chángcháng zuò shénme?**

B: 我常常跟朋友一起去饭馆儿吃饭。 **Wǒ chángcháng gēn péngyou yìqǐ qù fànguǎnr chīfàn.**

A: 你几点睡觉？ **Nǐ jǐ diǎn shuìjiào?**

B: 我有时候十一点睡觉，有时候十二点睡觉。 **Wǒ yǒushíhou shíyī diǎn shuìjiào, yǒushíhou shí'èr diǎn shuìjiào.**

Translation of Dialogue II

A: What time do you get up in the morning?

B: At 7:00. After I get up, I shower, and then go for breakfast. I go to work at 9:00.

A: When do you go to the cafeteria at lunchtime?

B: I go to eat lunch at 12:00.

A: When do you get out of work?

B: I get off duty at 5:00.

A: What do you usually do in the evening?

B: I often go out to eat at a restaurant with friends.

A: When do you go to bed?

B: Sometimes I go to bed at 11:00, and sometimes at 12:00.

day: 26

Opening Times

Day 26 continues to discuss the notion of time. In this lesson you will learn words for specific times and how to discuss habitual actions and actions that have taken and will take place in the past and future. There is also a pronunciation practicec section at the end of the lesson.

BUSINESS HOURS...

Stores and restaurants are open seven days a week. Government agencies, including banks and offices, are open Monday through Friday. Daily working hours are 8:30 a.m.–5:30 p.m., with a one- or two-hour lunch break around noon.

Grammar

Time words in a sentence

There are two kinds of time words in Chinese: words for specific times and words for time duration. In this lesson you will only learn words for specific times, such as now, morning, and 8:30. Examples of time duration words are one day and ten minutes.

Position of time words in a sentence

Specific time words always come before the verb in a sentence. The time word may come at the very beginning of the sentence, or it may come after the subject but before the verb.

Time words at the beginning of a sentence:

现在几点？ **Xiànzài jǐ diǎn?**	What time is it now?
晚上你常常做什么？ **Wǎnshang nǐ cháng-cháng zuò shénme?**	What do you usually do in the evening?
五点五分 我去找你。 **Wǔ diǎn wǔ fēn wǒ qù zhǎo nǐ.**	I will go to your place at 5:05.

Time words after the subject but before the verb:

你早上几点起床？ **Nǐ zǎoshang jǐ diǎn qǐchuáng?**	What time do you get up in the morning?
我十一点睡觉。 **Wǒ shíyī diǎn shuìjiào.**	I go to bed at 11:00.
我下午有英语课。 **Wǒ xiàwǔ yǒu Yīngyǔkè.**	I have English class in the afternoon.

Note that when the time word is interrogative, it is located immediately before the verb:

你早上几点起床？ **Nǐ zǎoshang jǐ diǎn qǐchuáng?**	What time do you get up in the morning?
晚上你什么时候睡觉？ **Wǎnshang nǐ shénme shíhòu shuìjiào?**	When do you go to bed in the evening?

Sequence of time words in a sentence

If there are two or more time words in a sentence, they appear in order from the broadest unit of time to smallest unit of time. For example, 11:30 in the morning will be 早上十一点半 **zǎoshang shíyī diǎn bàn** (literally: *morning, 11 o'clock, half hour*).

Specific time word + place + action

If you want to say that somebody is "doing something at some place at a certain time," the time words come before the place. For example: 我四点半在饭馆等你 **Wǒ sì diǎn bàn zài fànguǎnr děng nǐ** (literally: *I, 4:30, at the restaurant, wait for you*).

When telling time in Chinese, there is no need for a preposition such as 在 **zài** *(at)* before a time word. *"I go to bed at 11:00"* in Chinese is 我十一点睡觉 **Wǒ shíyī diǎn shuìjiào** (literally: *I, 11:00, go to bed*).

是 shì in time expressions

The verb 是 **shì** *(to be)* is not needed in time expressions, and it is usually omitted. If the verb is used, it appears between the topic and the number:

现在八点半。 **Xiànzài bā diǎn bàn.**	It is 8:30 now.
现在是八点半。 **Xiànzài shì bā diǎn bàn.**	It is 8:30 now.

A negative sentence must contain the negative form of 是 **shì**, which is 不是 **búshì** *(to not be)*:

现在不是八点半。 **Xiànzài búshì bā diǎn bàn.**	It is not 8:30 now.

Verb-object words as intransitive verbs

起床 **qǐchuáng** (to get up)
洗澡 **xǐzǎo** (to take a shower, to take a bath)
吃饭 **chīfàn** (to eat a meal)
睡觉 **shuìjiào** (to go to bed, to sleep)

Each of the words above is formed by combining a verb with an object. This verb-object structure, which is common in Chinese, functions as a verb.

Before/after

The word order of 以前 **yǐqián** *(before)* or 以后 **yǐhòu** *(after)* in a Chinese sentence is the reverse of that in English, where before or after precedes a time or event. In Chinese these words follow a time or event word, so that the English before 11:00 or after class becomes 11:00

以前 **yǐqián**, *(11:00, before)* or 下课以后 **xiàkè yǐhòu** *(class, after)*. The placement of 以前 **yǐqián** *(before)* or 以后 **yǐhòu** *(after)* in a sentence is always between one time or event and another time or event.

我十一点以前睡觉。 I go to bed before 11:00.
Wǒ shíyī diǎn yǐqián shuìjiào.

起床以后我先洗澡。 After I get up, I shower.
Qǐchuáng yǐhòu wǒ xiān xǐzǎo.

Often/sometimes

The adverbs 常常 **chángcháng** *(often)* and 有时候 **yǒushíhòu** *(sometimes)* are treated as time words, and thus their placement in a sentence is the same as time words.

Asking what time it is now

To ask the time in Chinese, say:

现在 几点？ What time is it now?
Xiànzài **jǐdiǎn?**

The structure for answering this question is the subject, followed by the time:

现在 七点五十分。
Xiànzài **qī diǎn wǔshí fēn.** Now it is 7:50.

Practice asking and telling the time in this sentence structure, using the times below.

2:00

4:15

7:30

5:05

6:45

9:10

8:55

Position of time words in a sentence

a. Time words at the beginning of a sentence.

When the time word is in the beginning of the sentence, the structure for asking questions is:

Time word	*Subject + verb*	*Interragotive*
下午	你 做	什么？
Xiàwǔ	**nǐ zuò**	**shéme?**

Literally, this means: *(In the) afternoon you do what?*

To answer these questions, place the time word, which becomes the subject, at the beginning of the sentence. This is followed by the verb and the object. For example:

下午	我 上班。
Xiàwǔ	**wǒ shàngbān.**

Literally, this means: *(In the) afternoon, I go to work.*

Practice asking and answering questions in this sentence structure using the time words and verbs and objects below.

Time word	*Verb + object*
上午	上汉语课
shàngwǔ	**shàng Hànyǔkè**
晚上	给美国打电话
wǎnshang	**gěi Měiguó dǎ diànhuà**
下班以后	去换钱
xiàbān yǐhòu	**qù huànqián**

b. Time words between the subject and the verb.

When the time word is between the subject and verb, the structure is:

Subject	*Time word*	*Verb + interragotive*
你	中午	做什么？
Nǐ	**zhōngwǔ**	**zuò shéme?**

Literally this means: *You (at) noon do what?*

To answer these questions, the structure is:

Subject	*Time word*	*Verb and object*
我	中午	休息。
Wǒ	**zhōngwǔ**	**xiūxi.**

I (at) noon rest.

Practice asking and answering questions in this sentence structure using the time words and verbs and objects below.

Time word	*Verb + object*
下课以后 **xiàkè yǐhòu**	去网吧 **qù wǎngbā**
下午 **xiàwǔ**	上课 **shàngkè**
晚上 **wǎnshang**	睡觉 **shuìjiào**

c. The interrogative time phrase is located immediately before the verb.

In this structure, the subject comes at the beginning of the sentence, followed by the interrogative time word, followed by the verb and object. For example:

你	几点	起床？
Nǐ	**jǐ diǎn**	**qǐchuáng?**

Literally, this means: *You (at) what time get up?*

The structure for answering is the same as for asking: subject, followed by time word, followed by verb and object. For example:

我	六点	起床。
Wǒ	**liù diǎn**	**qǐchuáng.**

Literally, this means: *I (at) 6:00 get up.*

Practice asking and answering questions in this sentence structure using the verbs + objects and the times below.

Verb + object	*Time*
睡觉 **shuìjiào**	10:30
吃早饭 **chī zǎofàn**	7:00
吃午饭 **chī wǔfàn**	12:00
上班 **shàngbān**	9:00
下课 **xiàkè**	3:45 p.m.

Specific time word + place + action

When you say that someone is doing something at some place at a certain time, the time words come before the place and the action. For example:

我	四点半	在饭馆	等你。
Wǒ	**sì diǎn bàn**	**zài fànguǎnr**	**děng nǐ.**
I	(at) 4:30	in the restaurant	wait.

Practice this sentence structure using the following time words, places and actions:

Time word	Place	Action
下午四点 **xiàwǔ sì diǎn**	在网吧 **zài wǎngbā**	上网 **shàngwǎng**
中午十二点 **zhōngwǔ**	在食堂 **zài shítáng**	吃饭 **chīfàn shí'èr diǎn**
晚上 **wǎnshang**	在宾馆 **zài bīnguǎn**	上班 **shàngbān**
上午 **shàngwǔ**	在银行 **zài yínháng**	换钱 **huànqián**

Before and after

Practice using 以前 **yǐqián** *(before)* and 以后 **yǐhòu** *(after)*.

Time words	yǐqián/yǐhòu	Subj.	Action
八点 **Bā diǎn**	以前 / 以后 **yǐqián / yǐhòu**	我 **wǒ**	洗澡。 **xǐzǎo.**
I take a shower before/after 8:00.			
七点半 **qī diǎn bàn**			起床 **qǐchuáng**
下课 **xiàkè**			休息 **xiūxi**
中午 **zhōngwǔ**			睡午觉 **shuì wǔjiào**
下班 **xiàbān**			去商店 **qù shāngdiàn**
找马丽莎 **zhǎo Mǎ Lìshā**			一起去餐厅 **yìqǐ qù cāntīng**

三点
sān diǎn
换钱
huànqián

去网吧
qù wǎngbā
买电话卡
mǎi diànhuàkǎ

Often and sometimes

常常 **chángcháng** *(often)* and 有时候 **yǒushíhou** *(sometimes)* are also used as time words. In questions using these words, the subject comes first, followed by **chángcháng** then the verb + object and finally **ma**? For example:

你	常常	去 饭馆	吗？
Nǐ	**chángcháng**	**qù fànguǎnr**	**ma?**

Do you often go out to restaurants?

To answer, start with the subject, followed by **yǒushíhòu**, followed by the verb (+ object). An answer to the question above could be:

我	有时候	去。
Wǒ	**yǒushíhòu**	**qù.**

I sometimes do.

Practice this sentence structure using the verb + objects below to ask the questions, and the verbs to answer.

Verb + object	Verb
换钱 **huàn qián**	换 **huàn**
去网吧 **qù wǎngbā**	去 **qù**
去商店 **qù shāngdiàn**	去 **qù**
买电话卡 **mǎi diànhuà kǎ**	买 **mǎi**
上汉语课 **shàng Hànyǔkè**	上 **shàng**

跟 gēn … 一起 yìqǐ …

The sentence structure for phrases with 跟 **gēn …** 一起 **yìqǐ …** *(to do something with somebody)* is:

Subject	gēn + person + yìqǐ	Verb	Object
我	跟朋友一起	吃	饭。
Wǒ	**gēn péngyou yìqǐ**	**chī**	**fàn.**

I eat with a friend.

Practice forming sentences in this structure using the people, verbs and objects below.

Person	Verb	Object
英国人	喝	咖啡
Yīngguórén	**hē**	**kāfēi**
王老师	去	换钱
Wáng lǎoshī	**qù**	**huànqián**
她	洗	衣服
tā	**xǐ**	**yīfu**
Liú小姐	去	商店
Liú xiǎojie	**qù**	**shāngdiàn**
马丽莎	上	课
Mǎ Lìshā	**shàng**	**kè**

Pronunciation Note: Differences between "j", "q", "x", and "zh", "ch", "sh"

Most English speakers need to pay special attention when learning Chinese to the differences in pronunciation between the initials "j," "q," "x," and "zh," "ch," "sh." You need to pronounce them accurately enough so a listener can distinguish between pairs such as:

jiā 家 *home* and **xiā** 虾 *shrimp*, or

quán 全 *complete* and **chuán** 船 boat

The sounds of "j," "q," and "x" are produced with the tip of your tongue placed behind your lower front teeth and with the upper part of your tongue just behind your upper teeth. Your mouth should be stretched wide with your lips tight.

The sounds of "zh," "ch," and "sh" are produced with your tongue pulled somewhat back and with its tip just touching the roof of your mouth.

Notice that the initials "j," "q," and "x" only take "i" or "ü" (spelled "u") as finals or the head of finals. For example:

jī 鸡 *chicken*	**jiā** 家 *home*	**juān** 捐 *to donate*
qī 七 *seven*	**qiā** 掐 *to pinch*	**quān** 圈 *circle*
xī 西 *west*	**xiā** 虾 *shrimp*	**xuān** 宣 *to declare*

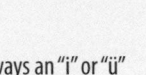

When you carefully listen to the sounds "j," "q," and "x," you will find there is always an "i" or "ü" included.

Pronunciation Practice

Read the following words aloud. Pay special attention to the differences between "j," "q," "x," and "zh," "ch," "sh." Check your pronunciation on the CD.

Pinyin	Chars.	English	Pinyin	Chars.	English
1. júzi	桔子	orange	**zhúzi**	竹子	bamboo
2. jūzi	锔子	cramp	**zhūzi**	珠子	bead
3. jiāng	姜	ginger	**zhāng**	张	to open
4. qiū	秋	autumn	**chōu**	抽	to take out (from in between)
5. qiáng	墙	wall	**cháng**	长	long
6. xùn	训	to train	**shùn**	顺	smooth

7. xuān	宣	announce	**quān**	圈	circle
8. zhuān	专	special	**chuān**	川	river
9. qúnzi	裙子	skirt	**Xúnzǐ**	荀子	surname of a Chinese philosopher
10. shàng	上	up	**xiàng**	向	toward

Each entry below has an initial sound and a final sound that combine to form complete words. Read the initial and the final sound, then read the full word. Check your pronunciation on the CD.

Group A:		Group B:		Group C:		Group D:	
j	**iǔ**	zh	**è**	y (i.	**īng**	z	**ài**
q	**ián**	ch	**ǎo**	w (u.	**ǔ**	c	**óng**
x	**iǎo**	sh	**āng**	yu **(ü.**	**án**	s	**ì**

Practice Pinyin by reading the following words aloud.

1. **jiājù** 家具 furniture
2. **shāfā** 沙发 sofa
3. **zhuōzi** 桌子 table, desk
4. **yǐzi** 椅子 chair
5. **shūguì** 书柜 bookcase
6. **cānzhuō** 餐桌 dining table
7. **diànshì** 电视 TV
8. **chuáng** 床 bed
9. **shuāngrénchuáng** 双人床 double bed
10. **chújù** 橱具 kitchenware
11. **guō** 锅 pot, wok
12. **bīngxiāng** 冰箱 refrigerator

day: 27

Telling the Time

Day 27 is about practising what you have learned in the last two lessons. Take the time to listen to the audio and to do the exercises to reinforce what you have learned so far.

A QUESTION OF AGE

*你多大了？ **Nǐ duō dà le?** (How old are you?) is a question for someone who is in the same generation as you. When asking people who are older than you, use the more polite 您 **nín** instead of 你 **nǐ**: 您多大年纪了？ **Nín duō dà niánjì le?"** (How old are you?). To ask the age of a child under ten, say: 你几岁了？ **Nǐ jǐ suì le?** (How old are you?). This is because **jǐ** 几 is usually used for numbers less than ten.*

Exercises

Exercise 1

Listen to the words on the CD, and then write the correct Pinyin spelling with tone marks for each word in the blanks below.

1. ....
2. ....
3. ....
4. ....
5. ....
6. ....
7. ....
8. ....
9. ....
10. ....
11. ....
12. ....
13. ....
14. ....
15. ....
16. ....
17. ....
18. ....
19. ....
20. ....

Exercise 2

Read and listen to the dialogue, and then answer the questions.

First review these new vocabulary words:

开门 **kāimén** (to open a door. 离 **lí** (from)

A: American 美国人 **Měiguórén**;

B: Chinese person 中国人 **Zhōngguórén**

A: 我要换一点儿钱。你知道银行几点钟开门吗？

B: 银行九点钟开门。

A: 现在几点了？

B: 现在八点。

A: 银行离这儿远吗？

B: 不远。就在书店旁边。

A: 好。谢谢。

B: 不客气。

Questions:

1. What time does this conversation take place? ....

....

....

2. What time does the bank open? ....

....

....

3. Why does the American want to go to the bank? ....

....

....

4. Where is the bank located?..

....

....

Exercise 3

Write the following times in Pinyin or Chinese characters:

2:00 p.m. ....

4:10 p.m. ....

6:15 p.m. ....

9:45 a.m. ....

10:05 a.m. ....

11:00 a.m....

8:30 a.m. ....

7:10 a.m. ....

12:00 p.m. ....

3:50 p.m. ....

5:55 p.m. ....

1:00 p.m. ....

Exercise 4

Fill in the blanks with the appropriate question word(s).

1. 你早上 .... 起床？

Nǐ zǎoshang..**qǐchuáng?**

2. 下课以后你做.. ？

Xiàkè yǐhòu nǐ zuò ....**?**

3. 你跟 .... 一起去商店？

Nǐ gēn .... yìqǐ qù shāngdiàn?

4. 晚上我去找你， .... ？

Wǎnshang wǒ qù zhǎo nǐ .... ?

5. 电话卡 .... 钱一张？

Diànhuàkǎ .... qián yì zhāng?

6. 厕所在 .... ？

Cèsuǒ zài .... ?

7. 你下午上班 .... ？

Nǐ xiàwǔ shàngbān .... ?

Exercise 5

To be able to communicate in Chinese, you will need to be able to talk about schedules. To practice, translate the following sentences into Chinese. Write the Chinese in Pinyin or characters.

1. **What time is it now? It is five to ten.** ....

....

2. **Shall we go to dinner together tonight?** ....

....

....

3. **What are you doing today? I am going to the Internet cafe after teaching English.**

....

....

4. **It is a quarter to four now. I will take a rest.** ....

....

....

5. **When do you go to bed everyday? I often go to bed at 11:00 p.m.**..............................

....

....

6. **Sometimes I take a shower in the morning, sometimes in the evening.**....................

....

....

7. **I go to class in the morning, and go to work in the afternoon.**....................................

....

....

8. **I get off work at 5:00 p.m.**...

....

day: 28

Calendars

Day 28 is all about expressing dates and moments in time. There is a big vocabulary booster section, as well as audio dialogues with native speakers to help you to continue to improve your Mandarin and to learn the words and phrases in context.

CHINESE CALENDARS

*Like much of the world, China uses the solar calendar (阳历 **yánglì**), based on the earth's rotation around the sun in 365 days. But the dates of traditional Chinese holidays are determined by the lunar calendar (阴历 **yīnlì**), based on the moon's rotation around the earth in 29 or 30 days, with 12 months a year, for a total of 354 days. Chinese solar calendars usually have the lunar calendar information in small print.*

Vocabulary

Key Expressions

今天星期几？
Jīntiān xīngqījǐ?
What day of the week is it today?

周末我洗衣服。
Zhōumò wǒ xǐ yīfu.
I do laundry on the weekends.

八月十号是我的生日。
Bāyuè shí hào shì wǒde shēngrì.
August 10 is my birthday.

我今年二十岁。
Wǒ jīnnián èrshí suì.
I am twenty this year.

New Words I • 生词一

Characters	Pinyin	English
今天	**jīntiān**	*today*
星期几	**xīngqījǐ**	*What day of the week?*
星期	**xīngqī**	*week*
星期二	**xīngqī'èr**	*Tuesday*
明天	**míngtiān**	*tomorrow*
星期三	**xīngqīsān**	*Wednesday*
每	**měi**	*every, each*
每天	**měi tiān**	*every day*
星期五	**xīngqīwǔ**	*Friday*
节	**jié**	*section, segment, period (of a class); festival, holiday*
钟头	**zhōngtóu**	*hour*
对	**duì**	*right, correct*
不对	**búduì**	*incorrect, wrong*

只有	**zhǐyǒu**	*only; only if*
星期一	**xīngqīyī**	*Monday*
星期四	**xīngqīsì**	*Thursday*
天	**tiān**	*day*
工作	**gōngzuò**	*to work; work, job*
外国	**wàiguó**	*foreign country*
公司	**gōngsī**	*company, corporation, firm*
做	**zuò**	*to be, to act as*
翻译	**fānyì**	*translator, interpreter; to translate, to interpret*
周末	**zhōumò**	*weekend*
星期六	**xīngqīliù**	*Saturday*
家	**jiā**	*home, family*
休息	**xiūxi**	*to rest*
洗	**xǐ**	*to wash*
衣服	**yīfu**	*clothes, clothing*
洗衣服	**xǐ yīfu**	*to do laundry, to wash clothes*
星期日	**xīngqīrì**	*Sunday*
看	**kàn/kān**	*to watch, to see; to look after*
电视	**diànshì**	*television*
可能	**kěnéng**	*may, might; possible*
电影	**diànyǐng**	*movie*

Dialogue I • 对话一

Roles

A: 周文 **Zhóu Wén;**

B: 马明 **Mǎ Míng**

A:	今天星期几？	**Jīntiān xīngqījǐ?**
B:	星期二。	**Xīngqī'èr.**
A:	明天星期三。我有中文课。	**Míngtiān xīngqīsān. Wǒ yǒu Zhōngwénkè.**
B:	你每天都有中文课吗？	**Nǐ měitiān dōu yǒu Zhōngwénkè ma?**
A:	不，星期三和星期五下午我有中文课，学中文。	**Bù, xīngqīsān hé xīngqīwǔ xiàwǔ wǒ yǒu Zhōngwénkè, xué Zhōngwén.**
B:	你每天上几节中文课？	**Nǐ měitiān shàng jǐ jié Zhōngwénkè?**
A:	两节。	**Liǎng jié.**
B:	一节课是一个钟头，对不对？	**Yì jié kè shì yí ge zhōngtóu6, duì búduì?**
A:	不。一节课只有五十分钟。	**Bù. Yì jié kè zhǐyǒu wǔshí fēnzhōng.**
B:	星期一， 星期二和星期四你都没有课吗？	**Xīngqīyī, xīngqī'er hé xīngqīsì nǐ dōu méiyǒu kè ma?**
A:	这三天我工作，我在一个外国公司做翻译。	**Zhè sān tiān wǒ gōngzuò. Wǒ zài yí ge wàiguó gōngsī zuò fānyì.**
B:	这个周末你做什么？	**Zhè ge zhōumò nǐ zuò shénme?**
A:	星期六在家休息,洗衣服。星期日看电视，也可能去看电影。	**Xīngqīliù zài jiā xiūxi, xǐ yīfu. Xīngqīrì kàn diànshì, yě kěnéng qù kàn diànyǐng.**

Translation of Dialogue I

A: What day is it today?
B: Tuesday.
A: Tomorrow is Wednesday. I have Chinese class.
B: Do you have Chinese class every day?
A: No, on Wednesday and Friday afternoons I have Chinese class; I study Chinese.
B: How many Chinese classes do you have each day?
A: Two.
B: Each class is one hour, is that correct?
A: No. Each class is only fifty minutes.
B: You don't have classes on Monday, Tuesday and Thursday, do you?
A: Those three days I work. I am a translator for a foreign company.
B: What will you do this weekend?
A: I will rest and do laundry at home on Saturday. I will watch TV on Sunday. I may go to a movie.

In the dialogue, 几 **jǐ** *(which, what)* is an interrogative used to ask for a date, time, or number:

几月 **jǐyuè?**	What month?
几号 **jǐhào?**	What date? What number?
几点 **jǐdiǎn?**	What time? What hour?
星期几 **xīngqījǐ?**	What day of the week?

When followed by a measure word, 几 **jǐ** is also used to ask the quantity of something. For example:

几个钟头 **jǐ ge zhōngtóu?**	How many hours?
几分钟 **jǐ fēnzhōng?**	How many minutes?
几天 **jǐtiān?**	How many days?
几年 **jǐnián?**	How many years?

每天 měi tiān + dōu + verb

In Chinese, 每天 **měi tiān** means *every day*. 都 **dōu** *(all)* is placed before the verb and emphasizes doing the same thing every day.

学 **xué** *(to study)* as a transitive verb can be followed by a noun, as in 学中文 **xué Zhōngwén** *(to study Chinese)* and 学英文 **xué Yīngwén** *(to study English)*. It can also be followed by a verb, as in 学数数 **xué shǔ shù** *(to learn counting)*.

节 **jié** *(section, length, segment)* is a measure word for *class periods*, *train cars*, and *batteries*. 一节课 **yì jié kè** means *one class period*.

When counting hours, use the measure word 个 **ge** before 钟头 **zhōngtóu** *(hour)*:

一个钟头 **yí ge zhōngtóu**	one hour
四个钟头 **sì ge zhōngtóu**	four hours

个 **ge** is also used with the more formal term
小时 **xiǎoshí** *(hour)*: 一个小时 **yí ge xiǎoshí** *(one hour)*.

分钟 **fēnzhōng** *(minute)* is used when counting minutes (duration of time).

休息 **xiūxi** *(to rest, to relax)* is an intransitive verb and thus cannot be followed by a noun, but it can be followed by a word or phrase of time duration:

休息十分钟 **xiūxi shí fēnzhōng**	to rest for ten minutes
休息一会儿 **xiūxi yí huìr**	to have a break (for a little while)

New Words II • 生词二

Characters	Pinyin	English
号	**hào**	*date*
几号	**jǐhào**	*What date (of the month)? What number?*
月	**yuè**	*month*
八月	**bāyuè**	*August*
生日	**shēngrì**	*birthday*
哪年	**nǎnián**	*Which year?*
年	**nián**	*year*
出生	**chūshēng**	*to be born*
生	**shēng**	*to give birth to, to be born, to grow; life; raw*
今年	**jīnnián**	*this year*

岁	**suì**	*year of age, year old*
多大	**duōdà**	*How old?*
四月	**sìyuè**	*April*
大	**dà**	*old* (when referring to age)
过	**guò**	*to pass, to cross; to celebrate, to spend (time); to go through*
过生日	**guò shēngrì**	*to celebrate a birthday*
明年	**míngnián**	*next year*
想	**xiǎng**	*to want, to think*
星期天	**xīngqītiān**	*Sunday*
昨天	**zuótiān**	*yesterday*
前天	**qiántiān**	*the day before yesterday*
后天	**hòutiān**	*the day after tomorrow*
上个	**shàng ge**	*previous, first part of*
上个星期	**shàng ge xīngqī**	*last week*
这个星期	**zhè ge xīngqī**	*this week*
下个	**xià ge**	*next, second, latter*
下个星期	**xià ge xīngqī**	*next week*
每个	**měi ge**	*every, each*
每个星期	**měi ge xīngqī**	*every week, weekly*
去年	**qùnián**	*last year*
上个月	**shàng ge yuè**	*last month*
这个月	**zhè ge yuè**	*this month*
下个月	**xià ge yuè**	*next month*

Dialogue II • 对话二

Roles

A:	Foreigner	外国人 **wàiguórén;**
B:	Chinese person	中国人 **Zhōngguórén**

A:	今天几号？	**Jīntiān jǐ hào?**
B.	今天八月十号。	**Jīntiān bāyuè shí hào.**
A.	明天八月十一号，是我的生日。	**Míngtiān bāyuè shíyī hào, shì wǒde shēngrì.**
B.	你是哪年出生的？	**Nǐ shì nǎnián chūshēng de?**
A.	我是一九八五年生的。我今年二十一岁了。你呢？你多大了？	**Wǒ shì yī jiǔ bā wǔ nián shēng de. Wǒ jīnnián èrshíyī suì le. Nǐ ne? Nǐ duō dà le?**
B.	我今年三十九岁。	**Wǒ jīnnián sānshíjiǔ suì.**
A.	你的生日是哪天？	**Nǐde shēngrì shì nǎ tiān?**
B.	我的生日是四月六号。我是在美国过的生日。明天我们在北京给你过生日。	**Wǒde shēngrì shì sìyuè liù hào. Wǒ shì zài Měiguó guò de shēngrì. Míngtiān wǒmen zài Beijing gěi nǐ guò shēngrì.**
A.	太好了! 谢谢!	**Tài hǎo le! Xièxie!**
B.	明年我也想在北京过生日。	**Míngnián wǒ yě xiǎng zài Běijīng guò shēngrì.**

Translation of Dialogue II

A: What day is it today?

B: Today is August 10.

A: Tomorrow is August 11. It is my birthday.

B: Which year were you born?

A: I was born in 1985. I am twenty-one this year. How about you? How old are you?

B: I am thirty-nine this year.

A: Which day is your birthday?

B: My birthday is April 6. I celebrated my birthday in the United States. Tomorrow we will celebrate your birthday in Beijing.

A: That's great! Thank you.

B: I also want to celebrate my birthday in Beijing next year.

day: 29

Making Conversation

Day 29 is all about the days of the week and expressing what has happened and is about to happen and making conversation in Mandarin. You will learn the days of the week, the months and how to read dates. You will also learn a little cultural information about Chinese birth signs.

CHINESE BIRTH SIGNS (生肖 SHĒNGXIĀO)

Twelve animals, representing the twelve Earthly Branches, are used to symbolize the year in which a person is born. Traditionally, it is believed that birth signs reflect one's personality and influence the choice of a spouse. When you look up your birth sign, remember to use your birth year according to the lunar calendar, which begins in late January or February of the solar calendar.

鼠 ***shǔ*** *(mouse)*	*1996*	*1984*	*1972*	*1960*	*1948*	*1936*
牛 ***niú*** *(ox)*	*1997*	*1985*	*1973*	*1961*	*1949*	*1937*
虎 ***hǔ*** *(tiger)*	*1998*	*1986*	*1974*	*1962*	*1950*	*1938*
兔 ***tù*** *(rabbit)*	*1999*	*1987*	*1975*	*1963*	*1951*	*1939*
龙 ***lóng*** *(dragon)*	*2000*	*1988*	*1976*	*1964*	*1952*	*1940*
蛇 ***shé*** *(snake)*	*2001*	*1989*	*1977*	*1965*	*1953*	*1941*
马 ***mǎ*** *(horse)*	*2002*	*1990*	*1978*	*1966*	*1954*	*1942*
羊 ***yáng*** *(sheep)*	*2003*	*1991*	*1979*	*1967*	*1955*	*1943*
猴 ***hóu*** *(monkey)*	*2004*	*1992*	*1980*	*1968*	*1956*	*1944*
鸡 ***jī*** *(rooster)*	*2005*	*1993*	*1981*	*1969*	*1957*	*1945*
狗 ***gǒu*** *(dog)*	*2006*	*1994*	*1982*	*1970*	*1958*	*1946*
猪 ***zhū*** *(pig)*	*2007*	*1995*	*1983*	*1971*	*1959*	*1947*

The days of the week

Until recently, the Chinese counted days only in months, not weeks. Then, at the beginning of the twentieth century, the concept of week 星期 **xīngqī** was adopted from the West. There are no special names for the seven days of the week in Chinese. Instead, the days Monday through Saturday are simply stated as 星期 **xīngqī** followed by a number from one to six, and Sunday is stated as 星期 **xīngqī** followed by 日 **rì** or 天 **tiān**. The literal meaning of 星期 **xīngqī** is star period.

English Day of week	Xīngqī + Number
Monday	星期 **xīngqī** 一 **yī**
Tuesday	星期 **xīngqī** 二 **èr**
Wednesday	星期 **xīngqī** 三 **sān**
Thursday	星期 **xīngqī** 四 **sì**
Friday	星期 **xīngqī** 五 **wǔ**
Saturday	星期 **xīngqī** 六 **liù**
Sunday	星期 **xīngqī** 日 **rì** / 星期天 **xīngqītiān**

Time description

the day before yesterday	前天 **qiántiān**
yesterday	昨天 **zuótiān**
today	今天 **jīntiān**
tomorrow	明天 **míngtiān**
the day after tomorrow	后天 **hòutiān**
last year	去年 **qùnián**
this year	今年 **jīnnián**
next year	明年 **míngnián**

Measure words in dates

You might have noticed 这三天 **zhè sān tiān** *(these three days)* and 这个周末 **zhè ge zhōumò** *(this weekend)* from the dialogue in lesson 28.When counting 天 **tiān** *(days)* or 年 **nián** *(years)*, there is no need for a measure word. For example:

三天 **sān tiān**	three days
两年 **liǎng nián**	two years

But when counting 星期 **xīngqī** *(weeks)* or 月 **yuè** *(months)*, the measure word 个 **ge** must be added before 星期 **xīngqī** and 月 **yuè**. For example:

三个星期 **sān ge xīngqī**	three weeks
两个月 **liǎng ge yuè**	two months

这个 **zhè ge** *(this)* indicates the current day, week, weekend, month, etc. Unlike English, a day in the current week can be modified by 这个 **zhè ge** regardless of whether that day is already past or is to come. 上个 **shàng ge** means *last*, 下个 **xià ge** means *next* and 每个 **měi ge** means *every*.

这个星期三 **zhè ge xīngqīsān**	this Wednesday
这个周末 **zhè ge zhōumò**	this weekend
下个周末 **xià ge zhōumò**	next weekend
上个星期 **shàng ge xīngqī**	last week
下个星期 **xià ge xīngqī**	next week
每个星期 **měi ge xīngqī**	every week
上个月 **shàng ge yuè**	last month
下个月 **xià ge yuè**	next month
每个月 **měi ge yuè**	every month

Months

The names of the twelve months are stated by simply combining a number from one to twelve with 月 **yuè** *(month)*.

English	Number +	月 yuè
January	一 **yí**	月 **yuè**
February	二 **èr**	月 **yuè**
March	三 **sān**	月 **yuè**
April	四 **sì**	月 **yuè**
May	五 **wǔ**	月 **yuè**
June	六 **liù**	月 **yuè**
July	七 **qī**	月 **yuè**
August	八 **bā**	月 **yuè**
September	九 **jiǔ**	月 **yuè**
October	十 **shí**	月 **yuè**
November	十一 **shíyī**	月 **yuè**
December	十二 **shí'èr**	月 **yuè**

The days of the month are stated by simply combining a number from one to thirty-one with 号 **hào** or 日 **rì** *(day)*.

一号 **yí hào**, 二号 **èr hào**, 三号 **sān hào**...三十一号 **sānshíyí hào**

Sequence of year, month, date

If the month is given, it will come before the day, so *January 1* is 一月一号 **yíyuè yí hào**. Just as you've learned with regard to telling time, the sequence of time words is from the largest unit of time to the smallest unit of time. So for dates, the sequence is year, month, day of the month. For example:

2004年1月1号下午5点 — 5 p.m. on January 1, 2004
èr líng líng sì nián yí yuè yí hào xiàwǔ wǔ diǎn

去年三月五号 — March 5 of last year
qùnián sānyuè wǔ hǎo

是 **shì** *(to be)* usually is omitted when expressing time, although it is necessary in a negative sentence with 不是 **búshì** *(to not be)*, for example:

今天星期一。 — Today (is) Monday.
Jīntiān xīngqīyī.

他十九岁。 He (is) nineteen years old.
Tā shíjiǔ suì.

今天不是八月十号。 Today is not August 10.
Jīntiān búshì bāyuè shí hào.

The sentence pattern "是 shì … 的 de"

This sentence pattern is used for emphasizing the time, place, or manner of an action or event that occurred in the past. For example, the following way of asking someone's age places special emphasis on the specific year:

你是哪年出生的？ What year were you born?
Nǐ shì nǎ nián chūshēng de?

我是1981年生的。 I was born in 1981.
Wǒ shì yī jiǔ bā yī niánshēng de.

The next example emphasizes the manner of an action:

我是坐车去的。 I went by bus.
Wǒ shì zuò chē qù de.

If the verb indicating the action or event is a verb-object combination, 的 **de** can be either placed between the verb and the object or after the verb-object, with no difference in meaning. For example:

你是在哪儿换的钱？ Where did you change your money?
Nǐ shì zài nǎr huàn de qián?

or

你是在哪儿换钱的？ Where did you change your money?
Nǐ shì zài nǎr huànqián de?

How to say the year

A year is stated digit by digit, followed by the word 年 **nián** (*year*):

一九八一年 **yī jiǔ bā yī nián** 1981
二00四年 **èr líng líng sì nián** 2004

What day is it?

To ask about days of the week in Chinese, begin the sentence with the subject, followed by the time word, followed by the interrogative, 几 **jǐ**.

今天	星期	几？	
Jīntiān	**xīngqī**	**jǐ?**	What day of the week is it today?

To answer this question, simply use the same subject, followed by the time word.

今天	星期一。	
Jīntiān	**xīngqīyī.**	Today is Monday.

Practice the days of the week, as in the example, using the subjects and time words below.

Subject	Time word
明天 **míngtiān**	星期五 **xīngqīwǔ**
昨天 **zuótiān**	星期三 **xīngqīsān**
前天 **qiántiān**	星期二 **xīngqīèr**
后天 (the day after tomorrow) **hòutiān**	星期四 **xīngqīsì**
六号 **liù hào**	星期六 **xīngqīliù**
十五号 **shíwǔ hào**	星期日 **xīngqīrì**
二十七号 **èrshíqī hào**	星期天 **xīngqītiān**

Measure words

When you talk about days (天 **tiān**) or years (年 **nián**), no measure word is needed. But when saying how many weeks and months, the measure word 个 **ge** is needed.

Practice saying how many days or years by saying the following numbers with 天 **tiān** or 年 **nián**.

Number	tiān	Number	nián
一 **yì** one day	天 **tiān**	一 **yì** one year	年 **nián**
五		三	
两		四	
九		十	
三十一		十五	

二十	一百
七十	六十

Practice saying how many weeks or months by saying the following numbers with 星期 **xīngqī**, *week* or 月 **yuè**, *month*.

Number	ge	week	Number	ge	month
一	个	星期	一	个	月
yí	**ge**	**xīngqī**	**yí**	**ge**	**yuè**
one week			one month		
三			两		
六			五		
十			十二		
四			七		
八			九		

Asking someone's birthday

To ask someone's birthday, say:

你	的	生日	是	几月几号？
Nǐ	**de**	**shēngrì**	**shì**	**jǐyuè jǐhào?**

What day is your birthday?

To answer this question, start with the subject (my, his, etc.), followed by the verb, then the date, for example:

我的	生日	是	五月 七号。
Wǒde	**shēngrì**	**shì**	**wǔyuè qī hào.**

My birthday is May 7.

Practice asking about and telling people's birthdays using the subjects and dates below.

Subject	Date
他	十月一号
tā	**shíyuè yí hào**
王小姐	八月六号
Wáng xiǎojie	**bāyuè liù hào**
你朋友	四月九号
nǐ péngyou	**sìyuè jiǔ hào**

中文老师 **Zhōngwén lǎoshī**	六月三十一号 **liùyuè sānshíyī hào**
英文老师 **Yīngwén lǎoshī**	十二月十五号 **shí'èryuè shíwǔ hào**

To ask someone what he does on a certain day, or at a certain time, use the following structure:

Time	Subject	Verb	Int.
周末 **Zhōumò**	你 **nǐ**	做 **zuò**	什么？ **shénme?**

Literally, this means: *Weekend you do what?* or, *What do you do on the weekend?*

Your answer would simply be the subject (I) followed by the verb and object to describe your activities.

我 **Wǒ**	洗 **xǐ**	衣服。 **yīfu.**	I do laundry.

Practice asking and answering the question *What do you do on ...?* using the times, verbs and objects below.

Time	Verb	Object	
星期三 **xīngqīsān**	上	中文课 **shàng**	**Zhōngwénkè**
星期二上午 **xīngqī'èr shàngwǔ**	教 **jiāo**	英语 **Yīngyǔ**	
星期日下午 **xīngqīrì xiàwǔ**	休息	**xiūxi**	
明天 **míngtiān**		去 **qù**	商店 **shāngdiàn**
今天晚上 **jīntiān wǎnshang**	看 **kàn**	电视 **diànshì**	
这个星期六 **zhè ge xīngqīliù**	看 **kàn**	电影 **diànyǐng**	
星期四上午 **xīngqīsì shàngwǔ**	去 **qù**	换钱 **huànqián**	
中午 **zhōngwǔ**		睡 **shuì**	午觉 **wǔjiào**

Pronunciation Note: Accurate pronunciation of "u"

It is very common for English speakers to mispronounce 五 **wǔ** with the "u" not long enough. Remember that for "u" in Pinyin, the English equivalent sound is "oo." For example:

Pinyin	Chinese	English
1. **wǔ**	五	five
2. **wūzi**	屋子	room
3. **wǔshù**	武术	martial arts
4. **tǔdì**	土地	land, earth
5. **gǔdài**	古代	ancient time
6. **mǔqin**	母亲	mother
7. **dǔchē**	堵车	traffic jam
8. **dúyào**	毒药	poison

Pronunciation Practice

Read the following words and phrases aloud, paying special attention to "u."

Pinyin	Chinese	English
1. **wūyún**	乌云	black cloud
2. **wūguī**	乌龟	turtle
3. **wūlóngchá**	乌龙茶	Oolong tea
4. **Wúxī**	无锡	(city name)
5. **wúhuāguǒ**	无花果	fig
6. **wúmíng**	无名	unknown
7. **wǔqì**	武器	weapon
8. **wǔlì**	武力	military force
9. **wǔyuè**	五月	month of May
10. **wǔxīng**	五星	five-star
11. **wǔfàn**	午饭	lunch
12. **kùzi**	裤子	pants
13. **wùhuì**	误会	to misunderstand
14. **wùlǐ**	物理	physics

15. **wùjià**	物价	(commodity) price
16. **gūlì**	孤立	isolated
17. **Tánggū**	塘沽	(place name)
18. **Zhūjiāng**	珠江	(river name)
19. **zūjīn**	租金	rent
20. **dúlì**	独立	independent
21. **dúshū**	读书	to study
22. **tòngkǔ**	痛苦	pain, suffering
23. **zǔguó**	祖国	motherland
24. **dùzi**	肚子	stomach

Read the following words aloud. These name of fruits, vegetables and food can help you to practice your pronunciation of Chinese while learning those terms that are used every day in China.

1. **shuǐguǒ** 水果 fruit
2. **lí** 梨 pear
3. **pútao** 葡萄 grape
4. **táo** 桃 peach
5. **lìzhī** 荔枝 lichee
6. **xiāngjiāo** 香蕉 banana
7. **píngguǒ** 苹果 apple
8. **júzi** 桔子 orange
9. **shūcài** 蔬菜 vegetable
10. **bōcài** 菠菜 spinach
11. **báicài** 白菜 Chinese cabbage
12. **tǔdòu** 土豆 potato
13. **biǎndòu** 扁豆 green bean
14. **xiǎocōng** 小葱 green onion
15. **qīngjiāo** 青椒 green pepper
16. **xīhóngshì** 西红柿 tomato
17. **shēngcài** 生菜 lettuce
18. **tiáoliào** 调料 seasonings
19. **yán** 盐 salt

20. **hújiāo** 胡椒 pepper
21. **báitáng** 白糖 sugar
22. **cù** 醋 vinegar
23. **jiàngyóu** 酱油 soy sauce
24. **guàntóu** 罐头 canned food, tin
25. **yóu** 油 oil
26. **làjiāojiàng** 辣椒酱 chili sauce
27. **shípǐn** 食品 food
28. **miànbāo** 面包 bread
29. **miànfěn** 面粉 flour
30. **mǐ** 米 rice
31. **miàntiáo** 面条 noodle
32. **bāozi** 包子 steamed stuffed bun
33. **jiǎozi** 饺子 dumpling
34. **rìyòngpǐn** 日用品 household items
35. **féizào** 肥皂 soap
36. **shūzi** 梳子 comb
37. **wèishēngzhǐ** 卫生纸 toilet paper
38. **jiǎnzi** 剪子 scissors
39. **xǐfàjì** 洗发剂 shampoo
40. **yáshuā** 牙刷 toothbrush
41. **máojīn** 毛巾 towel
42. **yágāo** 牙膏 toothpaste
43. **zhījiadāo** 指甲刀 nail clippers
44. **guāhúdāo** 刮胡刀 razor

Read the following words aloud. These words can help you to practice your pronunciation of Chinese while learning some job titles that are used every day in China.

1. **yóudìyuán** 邮递员 postal worker
2. **dǎgōngmèi** 打工妹 farm girl working as a laborer in a city
3. **xiǎoshígōng** 小时工 hourly paid housekeeper
4. **qīngjiégōng** 清洁工 janitor

5. **fù xiàozhǎng** 副校长 vice-president, deputy headmaster or headmistress
6. **zǔzhǎng** 组长 group leader
7. **xuézhě** 学者 scholar
8. **bānzhǎng** 班长 class leader
9. **yánjiūshēng** 研究生 graduate student
10. **yánjiūyuán** 研究员 research fellow
11. **xìzhǔrèn** 系主任 department chair
12. **jiémù zhǔchírén** 节目主持人 TV host
13. **biānjì** 编辑 editor
14. **shèyǐngshī** 摄影师 cameraman/camerawoman
15. **shīrén** 诗人 poet

day:30

Celebrations

Congratulations, you've reached the end of this course. By now you should be confident understanding, reading and speaking Mandarin and you should have a solid vocabulary. Well done!

TRADITIONAL CHINESE FESTIVALS

Lantern Festival *(元宵节* ***Yuánxiāojié****), on the fifteenth day of the Lunar New Year (in January or February), marks the end of the Spring Festival. People hang lanterns and eat boiled stuffed dumplings made of rice flour (汤圆* ***tāngyuán****).*

Qingming Festival *(清明节* ***Qīngmíngjié****), on April 5, is for mourning one's ancestors. Traditional activities include sweeping off the graves of ancestors, offering sacrificial foods, and burning pieces of paper that resemble money for the dead to spend in their world.*

Dragon Boat Festival *(端午节* ***Duānwǔjié****), on the fifth day of the fifth month in the lunar calendar (in April or May), commemorates the death of* ***Qū Yuán*** *(475–221 BC), the father of Chinese poetry. People eat sticky-rice dumplings steamed in lotus leaves (粽子* ***zòngzi****). Some areas also have dragon boat races.*

Mid-Autumn Festival *(中秋节* ***Zhōngqiūjié****), on the fifteenth day of the eighth month in the lunar calendar (in September or October), commemorates an unsuccessful rebellion against the Mongolian rulers of the Yuan Dynasty (1271–1368). It is a festival for family reunions. On the eve of Mid-Autumn Festival, after eating dinner people watch the moon while eating "moon cakes" (月饼* ***yuèbing****) and fruits.*

Exercises

Exercise 1

Read and listen to the dialogue, then answer the questions.

First review these new vocabulary words:

糟糕 **zāogāo** (terrible, unfortunate)
时间 **shíjiān** (time)
功课 **gōngkè** (homework)
快 **kuài** (hurry up)
什么时候 **shénme shíhòu** (what time)

A: 今天星期几？

B: 今天星期四。

A: 今天不是星期五吗？

B: 不是。今天不是星期五，今天是星期四。

A: 糟糕！今天我有中文课。我的功课还没做呢。

B: 你昨天为什么没做呢？

A: 昨天下课以后我去银行换钱了。回来以后又看了一会儿电视，就没做功课。

B: 今天你什么时候有中文课？

A: 今天下午两点我有中文课。现在几点了？

B: 现在是九点半。还有时间，你快做吧。

Questions:

1. **What day is today?** ....

....

....

2. **What class does speaker "A" have today and at what time?** ....

....

....

3. **Does he have any problems with the class?** ....

....

....

4. **What time does this conversation take place?** ....

....

....

Exercise 2

Write the seven days of the week in Pinyin or characters in the blanks below.

Monday ....

Saturday ....

Tuesday ....

Friday ....

Wednesday ....

Sunday ....

Thursday ....

Exercise 3

Write the twelve months of the year in Pinyin or characters in the blanks below.

January ....

November ....

July ....

October ....

February ....

December ....

June ....

March ....

May ....

August ....

April ....

September ....

Exercise 4

Write the month and date of the national day of Canada (July 1), the United States (July 4), the People's Republic of China (October 1) and Taiwan (October 10), in Pinyin or characters in the blanks below.

Canada: ....

United States: ....

People's Republic of China: ....

Taiwan: ....

Exercise 5

Translate the following phrases into Chinese and write them in Pinyin or characters in the blanks below.

1. **Monday morning** ....
2. **Thursday at 3:30 p.m.** ....
3. **July 4, 1776** ....
4. **May 1, 2001** ....
5. **October 1, 1949** ....
6. **Sunday afternoon** ....

Exercise 6

Fill in the blanks in each sentence, paying attention to whether a measure word is needed.

1. .... 年有 .... 月。

(one) **nián yǒu** **yuè.**

2\. .... 月有 .... 天。

(January) **yuè yǒu** **tiān.**

3. .... 星期有 .... 天。

(one) xīngqī yǒu tiān.

4. .... 星期三是 .... 月 .... 号。

(next) xīngqīsān shì yuè hào.

5. .... 年我是 .... 岁。

(this) nián wǒ shì suì.

6. .... 月我去中国。

(next) yuè wǒ qù Zhōngguó.

7. 我 .... 天有三节课。

Wǒ (every) tiān yǒu sān jié kè.

Exercise 7

To communicate in Chinese, you will need to talk about your schedule. To prepare, translate the following sentences into Chinese. Write the Chinese in Pinyin or characters.

1. Tomorrow is Friday. I have Chinese class in the afternoon. ....

....

....

....

2. Do you teach English on Tuesday and Wednesday? ....

....

....

....

3. December 15th is my birthday. I want to celebrate my birthday in China. ....

....

....

....

4. **I do laundry every Saturday and watch TV on Sunday.** ....

....

....

....

5. **I will go to the Bank of China to exchange money on Monday.** ....

....

....

....

Key to Exercises

Day 3

Exercise 1:

1. China **Zhōngguó**
2. Hong Kong **Xiānggǎng**
3. Singapore **Xīnjiāpō**
4. Sweden **Ruìdiǎn**
5. Korea **Cháoxiǎn**
6. Japan **Rìběn**
7. Switzerland **Ruìshì**
8. Canada **Jiānádà**
9. Spain **Xībānyá**
10. Scotland **Sūgélán**

Exercise 2:

1. **Xī'ān** 西安
2. **Wǔhàn** 武汉
3. **Nánjīng** 南京
4. **Guìlín** 桂林
5. **Chéngdōu** 成都
6. **Chángchūn** 长春
7. **Wūlǔmùqí** 乌鲁木齐
8. **Shényáng** 沈阳
9. **Shíjiāzhuāng** 石家庄
10. **Zhèngzhōu** 郑州
11. **Héféi** 合肥
12. **Nánchāng** 南昌
13. **Chángshā** 长沙
14. **Hángzhōu** 杭州
15. **Tàiyuán** 太原
16. **Fúzhōu** 福州

17. **Guǎngzhōu** 广州
18. **Kūnmíng** 昆明
19. **Guìyáng** 贵阳
20. **Nánníng** 南宁
21. **Lánzhōu** 兰州
22. **Xīníng** 西宁
23. **Lāsà** 拉萨 (Lhasa)
24. **Yínchuān** 银川
25. **Shēnzhèn** 深圳
26. **Sūzhōu** 苏州

Exercise 3:

Refer to the CD to check your pronunciation.

Exercise 4:

1. **Yīngguó** (England)
2. **Yángzhōu** (a city)
3. **Mr. Wáng**
4. **Wǒ** (I, me)
5. **Yuènán** (Vietnam)
6. **yě** (also)
7. **xuéxí** (to study)
8. **wèi** (hello)
9. **yī** (one)
10. **yuán** (¥1.00)
11. **yǒu** (to have)
12. **yīn-yáng** (the two opposing principles in nature)

Exercise 5:

1. **Yǒuyì Shāngdiàn** (Friendship Store)
2. **Hǎidiàn (**a district in Beijing)
3. **Gùgōng** (Palace Museum)
4. **Tiānānmén** (Square, Beijing)
5. **Tiāntán** (Temple of Heaven)

6. **Hóngqiáo Shìchǎng** (Pearl Market, Beijing)
7. **Xiùshuǐ Dōngjiē** (Silk Market, Beijing)
8. **Yíhéyuán** (Summer Palace)
9. **Chángchéng** (Great Wall)
10. **Shísānlíng** (Ming Tombs)
11. **dàshǐguǎn** (embassy)
12. **Pānjiāyuán** ("Mud Market," Beijing)

Day 6

Exercise 1:

1. **shíyī**
2. **shígī**
3. **qīshíyī**
4. **sānshíliù**
5. **wǔshíjiǔ**
6. **jiǔshíjiǔ**
7. **sìshísì**
8. **yìbǎilíngyī**
9. **bābǎiyìshíèr**
10. **yìbǎi líng sān**

Exercise 2:

1. 三加六是几？ **9 Sān jiā liù shì jiǔ.**
2. 十加十是几？ **20 Shí jiā shí shì èrshí.**
3. 七加七是几？ **14 Qī jiā qī shì shísì.**
4. 五十加五十是几？ **100 Wǔ shí jiā wǔ shí shì yìbǎi.**
5. 四十五加六十六是几？ **111 Sì shí sì jiā liù shíliù shì yìbǎi yìshí yī.**

Exercise 3:

1. 12
2. 64
3. 38
4. 57
5. 89
6. 96
7. 101
8. 224
9. 756
10. 984

Exercise 4:

6: **liù**

1: **yī**

7: **qī**

3: **sān**

8: **bā**

5: **wǔ**

9: **jiǔ**

10: **shí**

Exercise 5:

1. ◆◆◆◆ + ◆◆◆◆◆ = **9 sì jiā wǔ shì jiǔ** 四加五是九
2. ◆◆◆◆◆◆◆ + ◆◆◆◆◆◆◆= **14 qī jiā qī shì shí sì** 七加七是十四
3. ◆◆◆◆+ ◆◆◆◆ = **8 sì jiā sì shì bā** 四加四是八
4. ◆◆◆ +◆◆◆◆◆◆◆◆ = **11 sān jiā bā shì shí yī** 三加八是十一
5. ◆◆◆◆◆◆ + ◆◆◆◆◆◆◆ = **13 liù jiā qī shì shí sān** 六加七是十三
6. ◆◆◆◆◆ + ◆◆◆◆◆◆= **11 wǔ jiā liù shì shí yī** 五加六是十一
7. ◆◆◆◆◆ +◆◆ = **7 wǔ jiā 'èr shì qī** 五加二是七

Day 9

Exercise 1:

1. What did the foreigner want to do?	Exchange money.
2. What kind of currency and what amount did he want to exchange at the bank?	He wanted to exchange $200 into RMB.
3. What amount did he receive?	1,660 RMB
4. How much RMB equals one U.S. dollar?	8.20 RMB = $1.00

Exercise 2:

1. Which item did the American want?	That one.
2. How much did he pay the clerk?	2.50 yuan
3. What did the clerk say after he gave her the money?	OK.

Exercise 3:

1. **liǎng kuài**
2. **liǎng fēn**
3. **liǎng yuán**
4. **liǎng qiān**
5. **liǎng máo**
6. **liǎng bǎi**
7. **liǎng jiǎo**
8. **liǎng Měiyuán**

Exercise 4:

37 **sānshíqī**

56 **wǔshíliù**

94 **jiǔshísì**

27 **èrshíqī**

19 **shíjiǔ**

65 **liùshíwǔ**

12 **shí'èr**

73 **qīshísān**

100 **yìbăi**

109 **yìbăi líng jiŭ**

123 **yìbăi èrshísān**

176 **yìbăi qīshí liù**

Day 12

Exercise 1:

1. What does the foreigner ask for first? Steamed bread.
2. What else does the foreigner ask for? Rice.
3. How much is the total cost? 3.00 yuan
4. The change the foreigner receives back is 2.00 yuan

Exercise 2:

1. How many dishes does the foreigner order? Two.
2. How much is the total bill? 5.00 yuan

Exercise 4:

1. fish **yú**
2. chicken **jī**
3. noodles **miàntiáo**
4. beef **ròu**

Exercise 5:

1. Is this a beef dish?
   这是牛肉吗？
   Zhè shì niúròu ma?
2. I don't want this dish. I want that dish.
   我不要这个菜。我要那个菜。
   Wǒ bú yào zhè ge cài. Wǒ yào nà ge cài.
3. I would like egg-drop soup.
   我要鸡蛋汤。
   Wǒ yào jīdàntāng.
4. I also want four steamed buns.
   我还要四个馒头。
   Wǒ hái yào sì mántou.
5. I don't want any more, thank you.
   不要了，谢谢。
   Búyào le, xièxie.

Day 15

Exercise 1:

1. What did the customer ask the waiter first? What dishes do you have?
2. What did the customer ask the waiter after that? What kind of meat dishes do you have?
3. What order did the customer finally order? Lamb

Exercise 2:

1. What did the waiter ask the customer? What would you like to drink?
2. What beverage did the waiter offer? Beer, coke and tea
3. What did the customer want? A pot of tea

Exercise 3: free answers

Exercise 4:

1. What dishes do you have?
   你们有什么菜？
   Nǐmen yǒu shéme cài?
2. Two of us are vegetarians. Do you have vegetarian dishes?
   我们都吃素。有素菜吗？
   Wǒmen dōu chīsù.Yǒu sùcài ma?
3. Please bring us two glasses of beer, one cola, and one water. (来 lái).
   请来两杯啤酒，一杯可乐，一杯水。
   Qǐng lái liǎng bēi píjiǔ, yì bēi kělě, yì bēi shǔi.
4. We would like to order three dishes: one quick-fried beef with onions, one fish, and one vegetable dish.
   我们要三个菜：一个葱爆牛肉,一个鱼和一个素菜。
   Wǒmen yào sān ge cài: yí ge cōngbào niúròu, yí ge yú hé yí ge sùcài.
5. Miss, the check please. How much is it altogether? (一共 yígòng).
   小姐，买单。一共多少钱？
   Xiǎojie, mǎidān. Yígòng duōshao qián?

Day 18

Exercise 1:

1. **rìběn** 日本
2. **rènào** 热闹
3. **réngrán** 仍然
4. **róngyì** 容易
5. **ránhòu** 然后
6. **ràngbù** 让步
7. **rénkǒu** 人口
8. **rènwéi** 认为
9. **tūrán** 突然
10. **chuanrǎn** 传染
11. **róngrěn** 容忍
12. **ruǎnruò** 软弱
13. **zìrán** 自然
14. **huāruǐ** 花蕊
15. **zérèn** 责任

Exercise 2:

1. What is the rate for a call to the United States? 3.50 yuan per minute.
2. What is the rate for a call to Japan? 2.00 yuan per minute.
3. What is the cheaper way to call? Use a phone card.

Exercise 3:

1. 银行 **yínháng**
2. 服务员 **fúwùyuán**
3. 宾馆 **bīnguǎn**
4. 402 房间 **sìlíngèr fángjiān**
5. 打电话 **dǎ diànhuà**
6. 在不在 **zài bùzài**
7. 回电话 **huí diànhuà**
8. 告诉 **gàosu**

9. 不客气 **bùkèqi**
10. 您找谁 **nín zhǎo shéi**

Exercise 4:

1. 我买一张 IP 卡。 **Wǒ mǎi yì <u>zhāng</u> kǎ.**
2. 我换一百块钱。 **Wǒ huàn yìbǎi <u>kuài</u> qián.**
3. 你要什么菜？我要一个鸡，三个馒头。 **Nǐ yào shénme cài? Wǒ yào yí gè jī, sān <u>gè</u> mántou.**

Exercise 5:

1. 一共多少钱？ **Yígòng <u>duōshao</u> qián?**
2. 在哪儿买电话卡？ **Zài <u>nǎr</u> mǎi diànhuàkǎ?**
3. 你们有什么 菜？ **Nímen yǒu <u>shénme</u> cài?**
4. 请问，马丽莎在吗？ **Qǐng wèn, Mǎ Lìshā zài <u>ma</u>?**

Exercise 6:

1. How can I make a phone call to the United States?
   怎么给美国打电话？
   Zěma gěi Měiguo dǎdiànhuà?
2. What number should I dial first?
   我先拨什么号？
   Wǒ xiān bōshénme hào?
3. How much is it per minute to call the United States?
   给美国打电话多少钱一分钟？
   Gěi Měiguo dǎdiànhuà duōshǎo qián yì fēnzhōng?
4. That's too expensive. Where can I buy a phone card?
   太贵了。在哪儿买电话卡？
   Tài guìle. Zài nǎr mǎi diànhuàkǎ?

Day 21

Exercise 1:

1. **nǚlì** (努力)
2. **nǚshì** (女士)
3. **nǚxìng** (女性)
4. **núlì** (奴隶)
5. **Lǔ Xùn** (鲁迅)
6. **lǜshī** (律师)
7. **lǘzi** (驴子)
8. **lúzi** (炉子)
9. **fǎlǜ** (法律)
10. **mǎlù** (马路)
11. **fùnǚ** (妇女)
12. **mìlǔ** (秘鲁)
13. **fènnù** (愤怒)
14. **kǎolǜ** (考虑)
15. **bùjué rúlǚ** (不绝如缕)

Exercise 2:

1. The room number of the female foreigner is 302. True
2. The male foreigner's room is in good condition. False
3. The female foreigner needs towels and clean sheets. False
4. The attendant will send towels and change the sheets. True

Exercise 3:

1. towels **máojīn**
2. soap **féizào**
3. toilet paper **wèishēngzhǐ**
4. hanger **yījià**

Exercise 4:

1. I need one roll of toilet paper and three hangers.
   我需要一卷 (**juǎn** – roll) 卫生纸和三个衣架。
   Wǒ xūyào yí juǎn wèishēngzhǐ hé sān ge yījià.
2. My lamp is broken.
   我的灯坏了。
   Wǒde dēng huàile.
3. Who is it? Please come back later.
   谁？请等一会儿再来。
   Shéi? Qǐng děng yí huìr zàíi.
4. Please clean my room now. Could you change my sheets?
   请现在打扫我的房间。能换床单吗？
   Qǐng xiànzài dǎsǎo wǒde fángjiān le. Néng huàn chuángdān ma?
5. Please send one bar of soap and two towels to my room. I am staying in room 312. Thanks.
   请给我送一块肥皂，两条毛巾来。我住 312 房间。谢谢。
   Qǐng gěi wǒ sòng yī kuài féizào, liǎng tiáo máojīn lái. Wǒ zhù sì wǎ fángjiān. Xièxie.

Day 24

Exercise 1:

1. **tàijí** 太极
2. **zhīshi** 支使
3. **zhīshi** 知识
4. **shízǐ** 石子
5. **sīzì** 私自
6. **jīqi** 机器
7. **shísì búshì sìshí** 十四不是四十
8. **shí zhǐ bù yī** 十指不一
9. **jījí nǔlì** 积极努力
10. **shí shì qiú shì** 实事求是

Exercise 2:

1. What does the English person want? To find out something.
2. What is the English person looking for? The library.
3. On which side of the library is the movie theatre? The right side.

Exercise 3:

1. 商店旁边有书店。 **Shāngdiàn pángbian yǒu shūdiàn.**
2. 英文系旁边是教学楼。 **Yīngwénxì pángbian shì jiàoxuélóu.**
3. 邮局在银行旁边。 **Yóujú zài yínháng pángbian.**
4. 食堂旁边是七号楼。 **Shítáng pángbian shì qīhàolóu.**
5. 马路对面有中国银行。 **Mǎ lù duìmiàn yǒu Zhōngguó Yínháng.**
6. 厕所在书店后面。 **Cèsuǒ zài shūdiàn hòumian.**

Exercise 4:

1. Where is the bathroom?
   厕所在哪儿？
   Cèsuǒ zài nǎr?
2. Where is the English Department? It is behind the classroom building.
   英文系在哪儿？在教学楼后边。
   Yīngwénxì zài nǎr? Zài jiàoxuélóu hòubian.

3. How can I get to the Bank of China? Go straight, and then turn left.
   我怎么走中国银行？一直走，再左转。
   Wǒ zěnme zǒu Zhōnggó Yinháng? Yìzhí zǒu, zài zuǒ zhuǎn.
4. Is there an Internet cafe around here? The Internet cafe is on the left side of the gate.
   附近有网吧吗？网吧在大门左边。
   Fùjìn yǒu wǎngbā ma? Wǎngbā zài dàmén zuǒbian.
5. Is it far? How can I get there?
   远吗?我怎么走？
   Yuǎn ma? Wǒ zěnme zuǒ.
6. Excuse me, where is the bookstore? First go straight, pass the Bank of China, and then turn left.
   请问，书店在哪儿？先一直走，经过中国银行，再左转。
   Qǐng wen, shūdiàn zài nǎr? Xiān yìzhí zǒu, jīngguo Zhōngguó Yínháng, zài zuǒ zhuǎn.
7. Is the hospital across the street from the main gate?
   医院是在大门对面吗？
   Yīyuàn shì dàmén duìmiàn ma?
8. The post office is not far. It is over there.
   邮局不远。
   Yóujú bú yuǎn.

Day 27

Exercise 1:

1. 捐款 **juānkuǎn**
2. 句子 **jùzi**
3. 柱子 **zhùzi**
4. 完全 **wánquán**
5. 转变 **zhuǎnbiàn**
6. 猪圈 **zhūjuàn**
7. 请求 **qǐngqiú**
8. 顺利 **shùnlì**
9. 英雄 **yīngxióng**
10. 通讯 **tōngxùn**
11. 长江 **Chángjiāng**
12. 追究 **zhuījiū**
13. 水渠 **shuǐqú**
14. 权力 **quánlì**
15. 接触 **jiēchù**
16. 拒绝 **jùjué**
17. 出去 **chūqu**
18. 居住 **jūzhù**
19. 专制 **zhuānzhì**
20. 追求 **zhuīqiú**

Exercise 2:

1. What time does this conversation take place? 8:00 am
2. What time does the bank open? It opens at 9:00 am
3. Why does the American want to go to the bank? He wants to exchange money.
4. Where is the bank located? It is next to the bookstore.

Exercise 3:

2:00 p.m.	**xiàwǔ liǎng diǎn**	下午两点
4:10 p.m.	**xiàwǔ sì diǎn shí fēn**	下午四点十分
6:15 p.m.	**xiàwǔ liù diǎn yīkè**	下午六点一刻
9:45 a.m.	**shàngwǔ jiǔ diǎn sānkè**	上午九点三刻
10:05 a.m.	**shàngwǔ shí diǎn líng wǔ**	上午十点零五
11:00 a.m.	**shàngwǔ shíyī diǎn**	上午十一点
8:30 a.m.	**zǎoshàng bā diǎn bàn**	早上八点半
7:10 a.m.	**zǎoshàng qī diǎn shí fēn**	早上七点十分
12:00 p.m.	**zhōngwǔ shí 'èr diǎn**	中午十二点
3:50 p.m.	**xià wǔ chà shí fēn sì diǎn**	下午差十分四点
5:55 p.m.	**xiàwǔ chà wǔ fēn liù diǎn**	下午差五分六点
1:00 p.m.	**xià wǔ yì diǎn**	下午一点

Exercise 4:

1. 你早上<u>几点</u> 起床？ **Nǐ zǎoshang <u>jǐdiǎn</u> qǐchuáng?**
2. 下课以后你做<u>什么</u>？ **Xiàkè yǐhòu nǐ zuò <u>shénme</u>?**
3. 你跟<u>谁</u>一起去商店？ **Nǐ gēn <u>shuí</u> yìqǐ qù shāngdiàn?**
4. 晚上我去找你，<u>好吗</u>？ **Wǎnshang wǒ qù zhǎo nǐ, <u>hǎo ma</u>?**
5. 电话卡<u>多少</u>钱一张？ **Diànhuàkǎ <u>duōshao</u> qián yì zhāng?**
6. 厕所在<u>哪儿</u>？ **Cèsuǒ zài <u>nǎr</u>?**
7. 你下午上班<u>吗</u>？ **Nǐ xiàwǔ shàngbān <u>ma</u>?**

Exercise 5:

1. What time is it now? It is five to ten.
   现在几点？现在差五分十点。
   Xiànzài jǐ diǎn? Xiànzài chà wǔ fēn shí diǎn.
2. Shall we go to dinner together tonight?
   晚上我们一起去吃饭，好吗？
   Wǎnshang wǒmen yìqǐ qù chīfàn, hǎo ma?
3. What are you doing today? I am going to the Internet cafe after teaching English.
   你今天做什么？下英文课以后我去网吧。
   Nǐ jīn-tian zuò shénme? Xià Yīngwén kè yǐhòu wǒ qù wǎngbā.

4. It is a quarter to four now. I will take a rest.
   现在差一刻四点。我休息一会儿。
   Xiànzài chà yí kè sì diǎn. Wǒ xiūxi yí huìr.
5. When do you go to bed everyday? I often go to bed at 11:00 p.m.
   你每天几点睡觉？我常常晚上十一点睡觉。
   Nǐ jǐ diǎn shuìjiào? Wǒ chángcháng wǎnshang shíyī diǎn shuìjiào.
6. Sometimes I take a shower in the morning, sometimes in the evening.
   我有时候早上洗澡，有时候晚上洗澡。
   Wǒ yǒushíhou zǎoshang xǐzǎo, yǒushíhou wǎnshang xǐzǎo.
7. I go to class in the morning, and go to work in the afternoon.
   我上午上中文课，下午上班。
   Wǒ shàngwǔ shàngkè, xiàwǔ shàngbān.
8. I get off work at 5:00 p.m.
   我下午五点下班。
   Wǒ xiàwǔ wǔ diǎn xiàbān.

Day 30

Exercise 1:

1. What day is today?	Thursday
2. What class does speaker "A" have today and at what time?	He has Chinese class at 2:00 p.m. today.
3. Does he have any problems with the class?	He forgot to do the homework.
4. What time does this conversation take place?	9:30 a.m.

Exercise 2:

Monday	**xīngqīyī**	星期一
Saturday	**xīngqīliù**	星期六
Tuesday	**xīngqī'èr**	星期二
Friday	**xīngqīwǔ**	星期五
Wednesday	**xīngqīsān**	星期三
Sunday	**xīngqīrì/xīngqītiān**	星期日/星期天
Thursday	**xīngqīsì**	星期四

Exercise 3:

January	**yíyuè**	一月
November	**shíyīyuè**	十一月
July	**qīyuè**	七月
October	**shíyuè**	十月
February	**èryuè**	二月
December	**shí'èryuè**	十二月
June	**liùyuè**	六月
March	**sānyuè**	三月
May	**wǔyuè**	五月
August	**bāyuè**	八月
April	**sìyuè**	四月
September	**jiǔyuè**	九月

Exercise 4:

Canada:	**qīyuè yí hào**	七月一号
United States:	**qīyuè sì hào**	七月四号
People's Republic of China:	**shíyuè yí hào**	十月一号
Taiwan:	**shíyuè shí hào**	十月十号

Exercise 5:

1. Monday morning
   xīngqīyī shàngwǔ
   星期一上午
2. Thursday at 3:30 p.m.
   xīngqīsì xiàwǔ sān diǎn bàn
   星期四下午三点半
3. July 4, 1776
   yī qī qī liù nián qīyuè sì hào
   一七七六年七月四号
4. May 1, 2001
   èr líng líng yī nián wǔyuè yí hào
   二零零年五月一号
5. October 1, 1949
   yī jiǔ sì jiǔ nián shíyuè yí hào
   一九四九年十月一号
6. Sunday afternoon
   xīngqīrì xiàwǔ
   星期日下午

Exercise 6:

1. 一年有十二个月。 **yì nián yǒu shí'èr ge yuè.**
2. 一月有三十一天。 **yí yuè yǒu sānshíyī tiān.**
3. 一个星期有七天。 **yí ge xīngqī yǒu qī tiān.**
4. 下个星期三是三月十六号。 **xià ge xīngqīsān shì sān yuè shíliù hào.**
5. 今年我是二十岁。 **jīnnián wǒ shì èrshí suì.**
6. 下个月我去中国。 **xià ge yuè wǒ qù Zhōngguó.**
7. 我每天有三节课。 **Wǒ měi tiān yǒu sān jié kè.**

Exercise 7:

1. Tomorrow is Friday. I have Chinese class in the afternoon.
   明天是星期五。我下午有中文课。
   Míngtiān shì xīngqīwǔ. Wǒ xiàwǔ yǒu Zhóngwén kè.
2. Do you teach English on Tuesday and Wednesday?
   你星期二，星期三教英语吗？
   Nǐ xīngqī'èr, xīngqīsān jiāo Yīngyǔ ma?
3. December 15th is my birthday. I will celebrate my birthday in China.
   十二月十五号是我的生日。我想在中国过生日。
   Shí'èr yuè shí wǔ hào shì wǒde shēngrì. Wǒ xiǎng zài Zhōngguò.
4. I do laundry every Saturday and watch TV on Sunday.
   我每个星期六都洗衣服，星期日看电视。
   Wǒ měi ge xīngqīliù dòu xǐ yīfu, xīngqīrì kàn diànshì.
5. I will go to the Bank of China to exchange money on Monday.
   星期一我去中国银行换钱。
   Xīngqīyī wǒ qù Zhōngguó Yínháng huàn qián.

Vocabulary

Characters	Pinyin	English
B		
八	**bā**	*eight*
吧	**bā**	*bar, cafe*
吧	**ba**	*(to make a mild imperative, to imply agreement or a degree of certainty, to express unwillingness or hesitation)*
白	**bái**	*white; plain*
百	**bǎi**	*hundred*
班	**bān**	*class; shift; regularly-run*
半	**bàn**	*half, partly*
拌	**bàn**	*to stir and mix (with sauce)*
办	**bàn**	*to manage, to handle, to set up*
镑	**bàng**	*pound*
办公室	**bàngōngshì**	*office*
爆	**bào**	*to quick-fry; to explode*
八月	**bāyuè**	*August*
杯	**bēi**	*cup, glass*
北	**běi**	*north*
北京	**Běijīng**	*Beijing*
杯子	**bēizi**	*cup*

币	**bì**	*currency, money, coin*
边	**biān**	*side, edge*
表	**biǎo**	*form, chart*
别	**bié**	*difference; don't*
宾	**bīn**	*guest*
宾馆	**bīnguǎn**	*hotel, guesthouse*
冰	**bīng**	*ice, to freeze*
饼	**bǐng**	*fried bread*
拨	**bō**	*to dial*
不	**bù**	*no, not*
步	**bù**	*a step; to go on foot, to walk*
不对	**búduì**	*incorrect, wrong*
不客气	**búkèqi**	*You're welcome.*
不是	**búshì**	*No, it is not.*
不谢	**búxie**	*Not at all./You're welcome.*

Characters	Pinyin	English
C		
菜	**cài**	*dish; vegetable*
菜单	**càidān**	*menu*
餐	**cān**	*meal; to eat*
操	**cāo**	*to operate; exercise*
厕	**cè**	*toilet*
厕所	**cèsuǒ**	*bathroom, toilet*
茶	**chá**	*tea*
差	**chà**	*short of, wanting; to differ from*
常常	**chángcháng**	*often*
炒	**chǎo**	*to stir-fry*
炒鸡蛋	**chǎojīdàn**	*scrambled eggs*
炒鸡丁	**chǎojīdīng**	*stir-fried diced chicken with diced vegetables*
叉子	**chāzi**	*fork*
吃	**chī**	*to eat*
吃饭	**chīfàn**	*to eat a meal*
吃素	**chīsù**	*to eat only vegetables (vegetarian)*
出	**chū**	*to go out, exit; to appear*
初	**chū**	*beginning, elementary*
出生	**chūshēng**	*to be born*
床	**chuáng**	*bed*
床单	**chuángdān**	*bed sheets*

春	**chūn**	*spring*
此	**cǐ**	*here, this*
葱	**cōng**	*green onion*
葱爆	**cōngbào**	*quick-fry with green onions*
醋	**cù**	*vinegar*

Characters	Pinyin	English
D		
打	**dǎ**	*to make (a phone call); to hit, to beat; to play (ball)*
打电话	**dǎdiànhuà**	*to make a phone call*
打扫	**dǎsǎo**	*to clean, to sweep*
大	**dà**	*big, large, major; age*
大门	**dàmén**	*main entrance*
大学	**dàxué**	*university, college*
单	**dān**	*single, bill*
蛋	**dàn**	*egg*
道	**dào**	*road, channel*
的	**de**	*(function word)*
灯	**dēng**	*light, lamp*
等	**děng**	*to wait*
地	**dì**	*earth, locality, field*
第	**dì**	*(indicates an ordinal number)*
地区	**dìqū**	*area, region*
点	**diǎn**	*o'clock; (decimal) point; to choose, to mark*
店	**diàn**	*shop, store*
电	**diàn**	*electricity; electric*
电话	**diànhuà**	*telephone*
电话卡	**diànhuàkǎ**	*telephone card*
电视	**diànshì**	*television*

电影	**diànyǐng**	*movie*
丁	**dīng**	*cube, diced piece*
东	**dōng**	*east*
都	**dōu**	*all, both*
豆	**dòu**	*beans, peas*
对	**duì**	*right, correct; opposite*
兑	**duì**	*to exchange, to convert*
兑换单	**duìhuàndān**	*exchange form*
对面	**duìmiàn**	*on the opposite side, across the street*
多大	**duōda**	*How old?*
多少	**duōshao**	*How many? How much?*

Characters	Pinyin	English
E		
二	**èr**	*two*

Characters	Pinyin	English
F		
法学院	**fǎxuéyuàn**	*law school*
翻译	**fānyì**	*translator, interpreter; to translate, to interpret*
饭	**fàn**	*meal; cooked rice*
饭馆(儿)	**fànguǎnr**	*restaurant*
房	**fáng**	*room, house*
房间	**fángjiān**	*room*
肥皂	**féizào**	*soap*
分	**fēn**	*¥0.01, cent; minute*
分钟	**fēnzhōng**	*minute*
腐	**fǔ**	*bean curd; to decay*
附近	**fùjìn**	*nearby; in the vicinity of, closely*

Characters	Pinyin	English
G		
港	**gǎng**	*port; Hong Kong (short form of* 香港 **Xiānggǎng***)*
港币	**Gǎngbì**	*Hong Kong dollar (HK$)*
告诉	**gàosu**	*to tell, to inform, to let know*
个	**ge/gè**	*(measure word for people or things, and can be used to replace some other measure words)*
给	**gěi**	*to, for (when transferring something to someone); to give*
跟	**gēn**	*with*
工	**gōng**	*work; worker; skill*
公	**gōng**	*public, state-owned*
宫保	**gōngbǎo**	*a spicy, diced meat dish*
公司	**gōngsī**	*company, corporation, firm*
工作	**gōngzuò**	*to work; work, job*
瓜	**guā**	*melon, gourd*
馆	**guǎn**	*shop, hall*
贵	**guì**	*expensive, valuable, honored*
贵姓	**guì xìng**	*Your surname, please?*
国	**guó**	*country*
过	**guò**	*to pass, to cross, to go through; to celebrate; to spend (time)*
过生日	**guò shēngri**	*to celebrate a birthday*

Characters	Pinyin	English
H		
还	**hái**	*in addition, still, yet*
寒	**hán**	*cold*
汉	**hàn**	*Chinese*
汉语	**Hànyǔ**	*Chinese language*
好	**hǎo**	*good, well, OK*
好吧	**hǎo ba**	*OK, all right*
好吗	**hǎo ma**	*Is it OK? Shall we?*
号	**hào**	*number, size; date*
行	**háng/xíng**	*line, profession; to walk; OK*
喝	**hē**	*to drink*
和	**hé**	*and*
很	**hěn**	*very, very much*
红	**hóng**	*red; symbol of luck*
后	**hòu**	*rear, back, the latter; behind, after*
后边	**hòubian**	*back, rear*
后天	**hòutiān**	*the day after tomorrow*
护	**hù**	*to guard, to protect*
护照	**hùzhào**	*passport*
花	**huā**	*flower; to spend*
话	**huà**	*word; to talk*
坏	**huài**	*bad, broken, to become spoiled*

坏了	**huài le**	*to be out of order, to become spoiled*
换	**huàn**	*to exchange, to trade, to change*
黄	**huáng**	*yellow*
回	**huí**	*to return, to go back*
婚	**hūn**	*marriage; to wed*

Characters	Pinyin	English
J		
机	**jī**	*machine, engine; opportunity*
鸡	**jī**	*chicken*
几	**jǐ**	*How many?; a few, several*
加	**jiā**	*to add; plus*
家	**jiā**	*home, family*
假	**jiǎ/jià**	*false; holiday, vacation*
间	**jiān**	*room; between*
见	**jiàn**	*to meet, to see, to call on*
酱	**jiàng**	*soy bean sauce, sauce, jam; cooked in soy sauce*
教	**jiāo/jiào**	*to teach*
椒	**jiāo**	*hot pepper plant*
角	**jiǎo**	*¥0.10; corner, horn*
饺	**jiǎo**	*dumpling with vegetable and meat stuffing*
叫	**jiào**	*to be called, to call out*
教学楼	**jiàoxuélóu**	*classroom building*
鸡蛋	**jīdàn**	*egg*
鸡蛋汤	**jīdàntāng**	*egg-drop soup*
鸡丁	**jīdīng**	*diced chicken*
几点	**jǐdiǎn**	*What time?*
几号	**jǐhào**	*What date (of the month)? What number?*
街	**jiē**	*street*

节	**jié**	*section, segment, period (of a class); festival, holiday*
今	**jīn**	*the present, today*
今年	**jīnnián**	*this year*
今天	**jīntiān**	*today*
进	**jìn**	*to enter, to come in*
禁	**jìn**	*to forbid; prohibition*
京	**jīng**	*capital; Beijing*
经过	**jīngguò**	*to pass by, to pass through*
境	**jìng**	*border, territory, condition*
九	**jiǔ**	*nine*
酒	**jiǔ**	*liquor, wine*
桔	**jú**	*orange, tangerine*
局	**jú**	*bureau; gathering*

Characters	Pinyin	English
K		
咖啡	**kāfēi**	*coffee*
卡	**kǎ**	*card*
开	**kāi**	*to open; to set out; to turn on, to operate*
看	**kàn/kān**	*to watch, to see; to look after*
可	**kě**	*co(la) (first character of* 可乐 **kělè***); but; can, may*
可乐	**kělè**	*cola (short for* 可口可乐 **Kěkǒu Kělè***)*
可能	**kěnéng**	*may, might; possible*
可以	**kěyǐ**	*may, can; may be permitted to*
课	**kè**	*class, course*
刻	**kè**	*quarter of an hour, 15 minutes; a quarter*
块	**kuài**	*¥1.00 (colloquial form of* 元 **yuán***), dollar; (measure word for things in chunks or solid pieces); chunk*
筷子	**kuàizi**	*chopsticks*

Characters	Pinyin	English
L		
辣	**là**	*spicy, hot*
来	**lái**	*to bring; to come; to arrive*
了	**le**	*(indicates a change of situation or completed action)*
乐	**lè**	*(co)la (second character of* 可乐 **kělè***); happy*
冷	**lěng**	*cold, frosty*
冷饮	**lěngyǐn**	*cold drink(s)*
里	**lǐ**	*inside, inner; a Chinese unit of length*
凉	**liáng**	*cool; cold*
两	**liǎng**	*two; a few*
料	**liào**	*material, ingredient*
零	**líng**	*zero*
龄	**líng**	*age, duration*
留学生	**liúxuéshēng**	*student studying abroad, foreign student*
六	**liù**	*six*
楼	**lóu**	*multi-story building; story, floor*
路	**lù**	*road; route, journey*
绿	**lǜ**	*green*

Characters	Pinyin	English
M		
吗	**ma**	*(forms a question)*
马	**mǎ**	*horse*
买	**mǎi**	*to buy*
卖	**mài**	*to sell*
买单	**mǎidān**	*bill/check (in a restaurant or bar)*
马路	**mǎlù**	*road, street*
馒头	**mántou**	*steamed bread, steamed bun*
毛	**máo**	*¥0.10 (colloquial of 角* **jiǎo***); a surname*
毛巾	**máojīn**	*towel*
没	**méi**	*not; to not have (short form of 没有* **méiyǒu***)*
没有	**méiyǒu**	*to not have*
每	**měi**	*every, each*
每个	**měige**	*every, each*
每个星期	**xīngqī**	*měi ge*
每天	**měi tiān**	*every day*
美	**měi**	*beautiful; America (short form of 美国* **Měiguó***)*
美国	**Měiguó**	*United States*
美国人	**Měiguórén**	*American (person)*
美元	**Měiyuán**	*U.S. currency, dollar*
门	**mén**	*entrance, door, gate*
米	**mǐ**	*uncooked rice; meter*

面	**miàn**	*noodle, flour*
面条	**miàntiáo**	*noodles*
米饭	**mǐfàn**	*cooked rice*
民	**mín**	*people, citizen*
明	**míng**	*tomorrow, next; bright*
名	**míng**	*name; fame*
明年	**míngnián**	*next year*
明天	**míngtiān**	*tomorrow*
末	**mò**	*end; powder; last*

Characters	Pinyin	English
N		
哪	**nǎ**	*Which? What?*
哪个	**nǎge**	*Which? Which one?*
哪年	**nǎnián**	*Which year?*
哪儿	**nǎr**	*Where?*
那	**nà/nèi**	*that*
那个	**nà ge/nèi ge**	*that one*
那儿	**nàr**	*there*
奶	**nǎi**	*milk, breast*
男	**nán**	*man, male*
南	**nán**	*south*
呢	**ne**	*how about (you, this, that)?*
内	**nèi**	*inside, inner*
能	**néng**	*can; to be able to*
你	**nǐ**	*you*
你的	**nǐ de**	*yours*
你好	**nǐ hǎo**	*Hello! How do you do!*
你们	**nǐmen**	*you (plural)*
年	**nián**	*year*
您	**nín**	*you (polite form)*
您的	**nínde**	*yours (polite form)*
牛	**niú**	*cow*

牛肉	**niúròu**	*beef*
女	**nǚ**	*woman, female*

Characters	Pinyin	English
O		
欧	**ōu**	*Europe (short form of* 欧洲 **Ōuzhōu***)*

Characters	Pinyin	English
P		
盘子	**pánzi**	*plate*
旁	**páng**	*side; nearby; other*
旁边	**pángbian**	*side; beside, nearby*
朋友	**péngyou**	*friend*
啤	**pí**	*beer*
啤酒	**píjiǔ**	*beer*
片	**piàn**	*slice, thin piece*
瓶	**píng**	*bottle*

Characters	Pinyin	English
Q		
七	**qī**	*seven*
期	**qī**	*period; to expect*
起床	**qǐchuáng**	*to get up*
汽车站	**qìchēzhàn**	*bus stop*
千	**qiān**	*thousand*
签	**qiān**	*to sign; a label*
签字	**qiānzì**	*to sign, to affix a signature*
钱	**qián**	*money, cash*
前	**qián**	*front; forward; in front of; preceding*
前边	**qiánbian**	*in front, ahead*
前天	**qiántiān**	*the day before yesterday*
青	**qīng**	*blue/green/black*
请	**qǐng**	*please; to invite*
请问	**qǐngwèn**	*may I ask . . .*
去	**qù**	*to go; away (after a verb, indicating action directed away from the speaker); past, previous*
去年	**qùnián**	*last year*

Characters	Pinyin	English
R		
人	**rén**	*person, human*
人民	**rénmín**	*people*
人民币	**Rénmínbì**	*"People's currency," Chinese currency (RMB, ¥)*
肉	**ròu**	*meat*
入	**rù**	*to enter, to join*

Characters	Pinyin	English
S		
三	**sān**	*three*
三刻	**sānkè**	*three-quarters of an hour, 45 minutes*
商	**shāng**	*business; a surname*
商店	**shāngdiàn**	*a shop, store*
上	**shàng**	*first, upper; to go up, to get on*
上班	**shàngbān**	*to go to work, to go to the office*
上个	**shàng ge**	*previous, first part of*
上个星期	**shàng ge xīngqī**	*last week*
上个月	**shàng ge yuè**	*last month*
上课	**shàngkè**	*to go to class, to teach a class*
上午	**shàngwǔ**	*morning*
商学院	**shāngxué-yuàn**	*business school*
烧	**shāo**	*to stew, to cook, to roast*
勺子	**sháozi**	*spoon*
谁	**shéi/shuí**	*Who?*
生	**shēng**	*to give birth to, to be born, to grow; life; raw*
生日	**shēngrì**	*birthday*
什么	**shénme**	*What?*
十	**shí**	*ten*
时	**shí**	*time, the present time, hour*
是	**shì**	*to be (am, is, are, was, were); yes, correct, right*

室	**shì**	*room; office*
市	**shì**	*market; city*
是不是	**shì búshì**	*Is it? Are they?*
收	**shōu**	*to accept, to receive*
手	**shǒu**	*hand*
书	**shū**	*book, document; to write*
数	**shǔ**	*to count*
暑	**shǔ**	*heat, hot weather*
数	**shù**	*number*
双	**shuāng**	*double, twin, pair*
书店	**shūdiàn**	*bookstore*
谁	**shuí/shéi**	*Who?*
水	**shuǐ**	*water*
睡觉	**shuìjiào**	*to go to bed, to sleep*
睡午觉	**shuì wǔjiào**	*to take a noon-time nap*
丝	**sī**	*threadlike, silk*
四	**sì**	*four*
四月	**sìyuè**	*April*
送	**sòng**	*to send, to deliver*
素	**sù**	*plain; vegetable*
酸	**suān**	*sour*
酸辣汤	**suānlàtāng**	*hot-and-sour soup*
素菜	**sùcài**	*vegetable dish*

岁	**suì**	*year of age, year old*
所	**suǒ**	*place; (measure word for buildings)*
宿舍	**sùshè**	*dorm*

Characters	Pinyin	English
T		
她	**tā**	*she, her*
台	**tái**	*stand; (short form of* 台湾 **Taiwan***)*
太	**tài**	*too, excessively, extremely*
汤	**tāng**	*soup*
糖	**táng**	*sugar, sweets, candy*
糖醋	**tángcù**	*sweet-and-sour (things)*
天	**tiān**	*day*
条	**tiáo**	*strip; measure word for long, narrow things*
通	**tōng**	*to lead to, to go through; open*
头	**tóu**	*head, chief, end*
图	**tú**	*picture, map*
图书馆	**túshūguǎn**	*library*

Characters	Pinyin	English
W		
外	**wài**	*foreign country, the outside; external*
外币	**wàibì**	*foreign currency*
外国	**wàiguó**	*foreign country*
外国人	**wàiguórén**	*foreigner*
外教	**wàijiào**	*foreign teacher (short form of* 外国教师 **wàiguó jiàoshī***)*
外事处	**wàishìchù**	*foreign affairs office*
丸	**wán**	*ball, pill, pellet*
碗	**wǎn**	*bowl*
晚	**wǎn**	*evening; late*
晚饭	**wǎnfàn**	*dinner*
万	**wàn**	*ten thousand*
网	**wǎng**	*net, Internet*
网吧	**wǎngbā**	*Internet cafe*
往	**wǎng/wàng**	*to go; toward, in the direction of*
晚上	**wǎnshang**	*evening, night*
喂	**wèi**	*hello*
位	**wèi**	*place; position*
卫生纸	**wèishēngzhǐ**	*toilet paper*
文	**wén**	*literature; writing*
问	**wèn**	*to ask*

我	**wǒ**	*I, me*
我的	**wǒde**	*my, mine*
我们	**wǒmen**	*we, us*
五	**wǔ**	*five*
午	**wǔ**	*noon*
勿	**wù**	*don't*
午饭	**wǔfàn**	*lunch*

Characters	Pinyin	English
X		
西	**xī**	*west*
息	**xī**	*to rest*
习	**xí**	*to practice, to be used to; habit*
洗	**xǐ**	*to wash*
系	**xì**	*department (in a college)*
虾	**xiā**	*shrimp*
下	**xià**	*to go down, to get off; down, under, below; next*
下班	**xiàbān**	*to get out of work, to go off duty*
下个	**xià ge**	*next, second, latter*
下个星期	**xià ge xīngqī**	*next week*
下个月	**xià ge yuè**	*next month*
下课	**xiàkè**	*class is over, to dismiss class*
先	**xiān**	*first, before*
现	**xiàn**	*now, present*
现在	**xiànzài**	*now, present*
香	**xiāng**	*fragrant, appetizing*
想	**xiǎng**	*to want, to think*
小	**xiǎo**	*little, small, young*
校	**xiào**	*school*
小姐	**xiǎojie**	*Miss, Ms., young lady*
下午	**xiàwǔ**	*afternoon*
些	**xiē**	*some, a few; a little*

谢谢	**xièxie**	*thank you*
新	**xīn**	*new*
星	**xīng**	*star; a bit*
行	**xíng/háng**	*line, profession; to walk; OK*
姓	**xìng**	*to be surnamed; a surname, a family name*
性	**xìng**	*sex; nature; gender*
星期	**xīngqī**	*week*
星期二	**xīngqī'èr**	*Tuesday*
星期几	**xīngqījǐ**	*What day of the week?*
星期六	**xīngqīliù**	*Saturday*
星期日	**xīngqīrì**	*Sunday*
星期三	**xīngqīsān**	*Wednesday*
星期四	**xīngqīsì**	*Thursday*
星期天	**xīngqītiān**	*Sunday*
星期五	**xīngqīwǔ**	*Friday*
星期一	**xīngqīyī**	*Monday*
修	**xiū**	*to repair, to fix*
休	**xiū**	*to rest, to cease*
休息	**xiūxi**	*to rest*
洗衣服	**xǐ yīfu**	*to do laundry, to wash clothes*
洗澡	**xǐzǎo**	*to take a shower, to take a bath*
需要	**xūyào**	*to need*
学	**xué**	*to study, to learn; school, knowledge*

Characters	Pinyin	English
Y		
鸭	**yā**	*duck*
要	**yào**	*to want, would like, need*
也	**yě**	*also*
业	**yè**	*profession; estate*
一	**yī**	*one*
以	**yǐ**	*at, on, of, with, by; to use*
亿	**yì**	*billion (hundred million)*
一百	**yìbǎi**	*one hundred*
(一)点儿	**(yì)diǎnr**	*a little; some*
衣服	**yīfu**	*clothes, clothing*
一共	**yígòng**	*altogether, in total*
以后	**yǐhòu**	*after; later on, afterwards; after*
一会儿	**yí huìr**	*in a moment, shortly, for a little while*
衣架	**yījià**	*hanger*
一刻	**yí kè**	*one quarter-hour, 15 minutes*
姻	**yīn**	*marriage; in-law*
银	**yín**	*silver, relating to money*
饮	**yǐn**	*a drink; to drink*
英	**yīng**	*Britain (short form of* 英国 **Yíngguó***)*
营	**yíng**	*to operate, to run; to seek*
英国人	**Yingguórén**	*British person*

英文	**Yīngwén**	*English language*
英文系	**yīngwénxì**	*English Department*
英语	**Yīngyǔ**	*English language*
银行	**yínháng**	*bank*
饮料	**yǐnliào**	*drinks, beverages*
一起	**yìqǐ**	*together*
以前	**yǐqián**	*prior to; ago; before*
医院	**yīyuàn**	*hospital*
一直	**yìzhí**	*straight, straight on, continuously*
用	**yòng**	*to use*
由	**yóu**	*reason; through*
油	**yóu**	*oil, grease*
邮	**yóu**	*post; to mail*
有	**yǒu**	*to have*
右	**yòu**	*right; right-hand*
右边	**yòubian**	*right side*
邮局	**yóujú**	*post office*
有时候	**yǒushíhòu**	*sometimes, at times*
鱼	**yú**	*fish*
语	**yǔ**	*language, words*
元	**yuán**	*¥1.00 (the basic unit of money), dollar*
圆	**yuán**	*¥1.00 (formal written form of 元 yuán), dollar*
园	**yuán**	*garden*

远	**yuǎn**	*far away, distant*
月	**yuè**	*month*

Characters	Pinyin	English
Z		
在	**zài**	*in, at; to be in, to be at, to exist*
再	**zài**	*again, still*
再来	**zài lái**	*come again, come back*
早	**zǎo**	*morning; early*
早饭	**zǎofàn**	*breakfast*
早上	**zǎoshang**	*morning*
怎么	**zěnme**	*How? In what way?*
炸	**zhá**	*to fry in oil, to deep fry*
找	**zhǎo**	*to look for, to seek; to give change*
照	**zhào**	*to photograph; license*
这	**zhè/zhèi**	*this*
这边	**zhèbian**	*this side, over here*
这个	**zhè ge/ zhèi ge**	*this one; this*
这个星期	**zhè ge xīngqī**	*this week*
这个月	**zhè ge yuè**	*this month*
蒸	**zhēng**	*to steam*
正	**zhēng/zhèng**	*first (in lunar calendar); upright; main*
证	**zhèng**	*certification, proof; to prove*
这儿	**zhèr**	*here*
这些	**zhèxiē**	*these*
汁	**zhī**	*juice*

直	**zhí**	*straight; vertical; frank*
职	**zhí**	*job, position*
止	**zhǐ**	*to prohibit, to stop*
址	**zhǐ**	*location, site*
只有	**zhǐyǒu**	*only; only if*
中	**zhōng**	*middle; China (short form of* 中国 **Zhōngguó***)*
钟	**zhōng**	*clock, o'clock*
中国	**Zhōngguó**	*China*
中国 银行	**Zhōngguó Yínháng**	*Bank of China*
中间	**zhōngjiān**	*middle, center; in between*
钟头	**zhōngtóu**	*hour*
中文	**Zhōngwén**	*Chinese language*
中文系	**zhōngwénxì**	*Chinese Department*
中午	**zhōngwǔ**	*noon*
周	**zhōu**	*week; cycle*
周末	**zhōumò**	*weekend*
猪	**zhū**	*pig*
住	**zhù**	*to live, to stay*
转	**zhuǎn/ zhuàn**	*to turn; to change; to rotate*
猪肉	**zhūròu**	*pork*
子	**zǐ**	*son; small; seed*
自	**zì**	*self; from*
走	**zǒu**	*to walk, to go, to leave*